Discover U Part II
"Dream Doers"

Dederick D. Woodard

Dream Doers

Copyright ©2019 Dederick D. Woodard and Dederick Woodard Inc.

All rights reserved. No part of this book may be reproduced, stored in retrieval system or transmitted in any form or by any means without the prior written permission of Dederick Woodard Inc. and Dederick D. Woodard. Except by a reviewer who may quote brief passages in a review to be printed in a newspaper, magazine or journal.

DEDICATION

This book is dedicated to you being real, it's dedicated to you being true, it's dedicated to a life of living dreams, it's dedicated to the courageous you.

Dream Doers

CONTENTS

	Acknowledgments	i
1	The Power of Sound	Chapter 1
2	The Power of Sight	Chapter 2
3	The Power of Action	Chapter 3
4	The Triple "P" Effect	Chapter 4
5	Second Time Around	Chapter 5
6	A Higher Vibration	Chapter 6
7	Transforming Transmissions	Chapter 7
8	Walking In Perfection	Chapter 8
9	Sowing Greatness Forward	Chapter 9
10	About the Author	Chapter 10

Dream Doers

ACKNOWLEDGMENTS

I acknowledge "you," for having a desire, and that you want to become more than just a dreamer. I acknowledge you and all your resources that you are dedicating to connect to, in hope that you will become aware of them all to utilize them on purpose and with a purpose. I acknowledge: Your Hope, Your Faith and Your Love. Your Hope to receive, Your Faith to take action, and Your Love to give back what was given to you that which now operates within you.

Dream Doers

CHAPTER 1
THE POWER OF SOUND

This is the part where I ask you to picture a box. Then I would like you to picture that you are in that box, and that box has a door. The door in the box that you are in has a key, and the key is hope. To turn that key you need faith. Now, faith to me is using your imagination correctly to transform your dream from within your mind to around you within your moment to become apart of your life. From nothing to something, or shall I say from nowhere to somewhere!

(James 2:18 Kings James Version) "Yea, a man may say, Thou hast faith, and I have works: shew me your faith without works, and I will show you my faith by my works."

It's like a fish being in a bowl and dreaming of existing in a bigger bowl, and manifesting effort with the wisdom to make it possible. It, meaning sound became something that was more than heard, it was manifested! Somehow the sound in your head escaped your mouth and found strength to build what it was saying. **You know,**

sometimes we cannot stop some dreams, because they are too determined. They find away even when it seems to be no way.

Some say that I am a dreamer, because sometimes I say things that they cannot imagine me doing. I have come to realize that their imagination and my imagination, are like two different worlds, we just spin differently around the sun but we do both spin. Remember that box we talked about in the beginning, because people will always try to put you in one (a box). Realize this, they can not put you in a box if they see that you have already placed yourself in a box. **I say box yourself in your dreams, and use your faith to open the doors to all your hopes and see where in your dreams those doors lead.**

Now, when you get there hear, and become aware of all the things that can connect to your dreams. Take notes, to ensure that you can know what to listen to, and also allow yourself the opportunity to understand what you have chosen to focus on. Have you ever considered this? "An undivided light is called a laser, and it can penetrate whatever it chose to focus on if it becomes the right kind of light." A flashlight can illuminate a dark area to expose a path. Wow! A penetrating laser or a shining flashlight are both types of lights, now both are needed and it takes understanding to know when to apply which type of light if you want to acquire your goals.

Awareness to me is noticing, connecting, and conversing with something on purpose and with purpose. You know like; putting toothpaste on your toothbrush with intent to brush your teeth? Putting on your running shoes to go running? Going to the library to study? Moving with a focus with the intentions to manifest! Going to a party to party!!! Yes, it's okay to develop expectations, we just need to know what we can expect out of what? You know you go to the gas station and expect them to have gas. Now, every now and then some do run out but we kind of know that we can count on the gas station to have that gas. That's what we need to take the time to do, and to do meaning to know what to depend on when it comes to our dreams. Are you as aware to the resources required to assist you in manifesting your dreams? I know that I can know more and do better? Hey, I am just keeping it real, believe that, and you might can know more and do better yourself. Now, we both need the courage to step out of our fish bowl to get into the fishbowl of our dreams.

Though it might seem impossible for some, but everything is not impossible for all. For those who say I can and put forth effort, will develop the ability. Now, if we combined that ability, with what some call potential with some willingness, all type of possibilities become possible. Repeat after me, well what I mean is to say what's in parenthesis (No Limits, No Boundaries). Like the little train that could, tell yourself "I think I can, I think I can, I think I can!" I read in the bible that, "as a man thinks so is he" Proverbs 23:7, so if you can get your mind to agree with your thoughts and your thoughts to agree with your actions there are no limits! You can and you will reach the bowl of your dreams!   What do you think about you? How do you feel about yourself and the desires that you have? Do you take the time to hear yourself? Are you aware of what's really going on with you?

Okay, what's one thing about your lifestyle that you can do better? Now that question is a starter question, but here is a question I would love for you to answer at least 3 to 5 times a day: <u>"What do you do good that you would love to do great?"</u> Its a head buster right? Because now we have to identify with that door of hope, and we have to consider where we would like for it to take us. Are you aware of your hopes, can you find those doors the doors that matter to you? Do you have the faith to unlock them? Because hope is believing that you can; which is being willing, and faith will release the ability through your effort as you submit to the ones whom are walking in the dreams that you dared to dream. We must listen to faith, yes apply undivided attention. We must hear and listen, be and become aware and apply undivided attention if we are to manifest. As we can see in the image about where the fish is upgrading its dream by connecting to what it has become aware of. It has put forth the effort and launched towards the vision and made the vision of its destination its destiny.

Now as we all know that to exist in your destiny you must apply discipline. Sound is something that makes enough noise until you hear it, then it desires to acquires your attention until it receives it undivided to ensure that you are listening. You see I learned a little secret about sound, it wants to get your attention until it matters. It knows that it matters when it becomes matter, or shall I say manifest in your life. So again I ask you what do you say to yourself about your dreams? As we think so are we, well what are we thinking? If you were the fish, and your life now is represented by the little bowl. The life you desire is the bigger bowl; my question to you is do you think that you can get that reality out of your head and into your moment?

You can prove sound right, or you can prove sound wrong, the choice is up to you. A sound wave is represented by a half of circle going above a point and below a point, and if you place those two halves together it will produce a circle. One half can be considered as all the joy and the other can be perceived as all the challenges. One pours into you and the other situation requires you to pour into it. And if you somehow master this dance called by some a frequency, others might have something they can tune into for inspiration and hope. Imagine that your will to press until you produce, presents a perspective that transforms someone into their destiny. Now, do not get it twisted what you are doing is for you, but it is also for those who see you that you know see you and for those who you don't know that see you too.

It's like they are watching their favorite movie and the one, that underdog that they have been praying for, has somehow or someway made what they thought was impossible possible. You know, "Ex nihilo" to create something from nothing, right? Sound seems like nothing until you become aware of it. What you are aware of seems like nothing until you focus on it in an undivided way because you desired to listen, what you knew was nothing until you chose to apply it and have an experience. Each time you experienced the reality of "Ex nihilo" because you were willing to allow something to manifest out of nothing. I said all that to say this, beauty is in the eye of the beholder, the value is there for those who can comprehend. To see value or beauty in anything, we must first grasp it mentally, which displays that we understand, then and only then will it be possible for us to fully maximize the opportunities before us. Again with the fish, most might just see two bowls, but understanding will reveal that it is more there than meets the regular eye. Understanding the value in what the two bowls are revealing, will expose your story within their presentation. So transform and be transformed to ensure your perspective is your experience. It seems impossible for some, but everything is not impossible for all. For those who say I can and put forth effort, will develop the ability.

Remember,

That Sound,

Brings with it,

<u>Awareness</u>!

So,

listen on

"PURPOSE"

and with

"PURPOSE!"

CHAPTER 2
THE POWER OF SIGHT

Sight, to see or not to see that is the question! Can you see? Can you see what you need when it comes to your dreams? Who can see past something that they do not understand? How can you see past something that you do not understand? Good questions can produce good answers, and great questions can produce great answers. Do you know how to identify the difference between the good ones and the great ones, and ones meaning questions?

The right questions will allow you to see your

challenges better. The right questions will allow you access to know the needed resources, and we all plug into what we know. It's as if you have assignments for your dreams, and you find yourself in need of comprehension to maximize your efforts. You see, to know if you correctly see your dream, to bring it to pass, you must do a dream inventory. Now to do this you must find those that are living your dream, and focus on what they see, and focus on what you need to not only exist in your dream, but to sustain yourself within your dream. To see correctly we must create an inventory checklist as seen below.

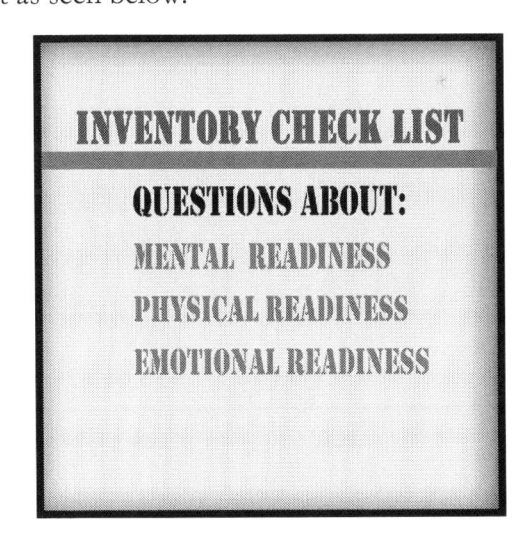

INVENTORY CHECK LIST

QUESTIONS ABOUT:
MENTAL READINESS
PHYSICAL READINESS
EMOTIONAL READINESS

An inventory checklist is used to properly evaluate what is required to see correctly. Just as a grocery list equips you to see correctly when going to the store. It prepares you to expect the things that will assist you in manifesting your dreams, and I know you heard this before, "if you can see it then you can do it!"

That's what this list empowers you to do. If utilized correctly a desire can become an experience. Now, people who can see right knows what questions to ask, either because of personal experiences or through observation. As we can see here it is about asking the right question when dealing with being ready, because we have all heard that when preparation meets opportunity success will be experienced. Let's get ready to rumble with success!

Preparation + Opportunity = Success

> **INVENTORY CHECK LIST**
>
> **QUESTIONS ABOUT:**
> MENTAL READINESS ✓
> PHYSICAL READINESS
> EMOTIONAL READINESS

The first thing on our inventory checklist is dealing with questions about "Mental Readiness." Remember that as a man thinks so is he, so we must develop questions that address, empower and equip how we think thus addressing who we are. Watching the right question being asked and learning to ask the right questions that address our mind being ready will assist us in <u>utilizing the tool that we use to see in our mind called our imagination.</u>

Now, the way we observe our atmosphere will change, and by equipping our mind to increase its level of readiness, we will enhance how we process the atmospheres of world around us. By learning to develop this method and applying it on purpose to transcend our collected data, allowing us to process that data with purpose in relation to our dreams. This deals with what I like to call your "will" to do. Now the "will" to me has at least two parts to it that have transformed my life, and I would like to take some time to focus on these parts to break down the will into these two parts for this teaching. Part 1 deals with what we have been discussing which is "Mental Readiness" and "Emotional Readiness."

We will address the Part 2 of the "will" when we get to the "Emotional Readiness" part. Now, the Part 1 of the will deals with "Mental Readiness," and the main question is: "DO YOU BELIEVE?" It's not about making a believer out of me, but in this case it's about making a believer out of yourself! You see, we all know that if you do not believe it you cannot do it, and it has been proven time and time again. Have you ever heard about the story about the fleas in the cup with the glass top? Well, one day a man decided to breed some fleas and each time he did the fleas would jump out of the cup and get away. So after his third time trying he went for professional help. The professional help said, "You must always keep a clear top over your cup to train their mind to not jump higher than this level which is the level of the clear cup." The man ask, "how is that going to train them?" The professional responded, "The ones that are in the cup will try to jump out and when they jump out they will bump their heads.

Now, bumping their heads will do two things: one it will teach them that trying to do this hurts, and two to teach this concepts to the others so they will not try. After about 6 to 8 weeks you will be able to take the clear lid off and they will not jump out of the cup, because they would have programmed themselves to only jump so far up." So, I said that to say this again,

"DO YOU BELIEVE?" Do you believe that you can jump out of something that everyone else has been programmed not to jump out of? So, equip your mind with questions for those who have done what some say is the impossible and jumped out. Believe!

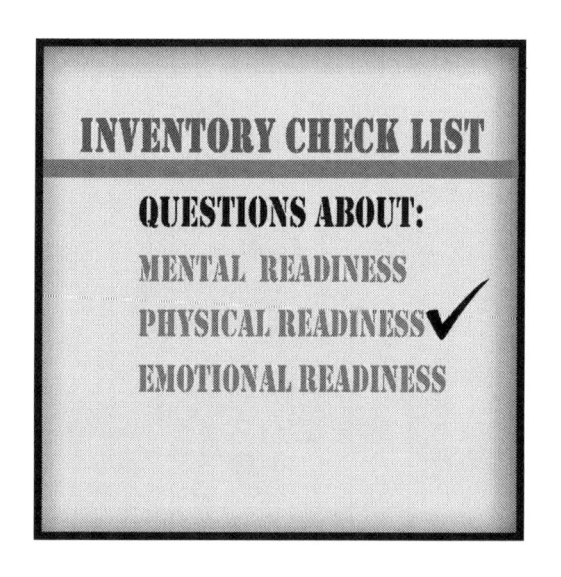

INVENTORY CHECK LIST

QUESTIONS ABOUT:
MENTAL READINESS
PHYSICAL READINESS ✓
EMOTIONAL READINESS

Before we get to Part 2 of the "will" we must address what I call: "The Can Concept," which deals with "Physical Readiness." Questions like: Can I do it? Am I strong enough? Am I enough? How can I become enough? Who do I know is enough? Who do I know that can? Who do I know that has done what I am attempting to do? We must tell ourselves to find them and weigh ourselves to know if we are enough to at least balance the scales. Because to know is motivation, and motivation can get you moving. You know, everything in motion stays in motion, a great journey begins with a step, so what's going to get us stepping? Do I need to do some push-ups, do I need to stretch, what do I need to do to get ready to move? These are the types of physical question we need to ask to connect actions with our believing. Yes, I say connecting your belief with realistic concepts will make it a lot easier to connect belief with works. Now knowing that I have a chance to develop or become and that is like having the fuel to the fire of my desires, and every fire needs fuel if we want it to burn past the finish line.

INVENTORY CHECK LIST

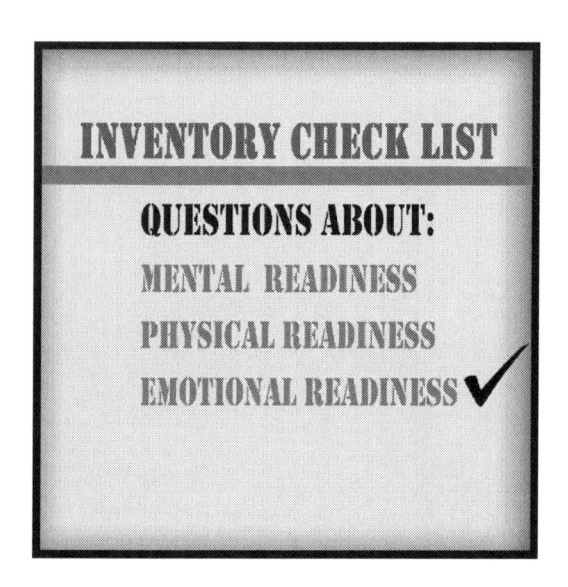

QUESTIONS ABOUT:
MENTAL READINESS
PHYSICAL READINESS
EMOTIONAL READINESS ✓

Part 2 of the "will," "Emotional Readiness" focuses on how this desire makes me feel. Well, doing something will make you feel some kind of way whether you want it to or not that's just the purpose of emotions. I was watching the movie "The Matrix Reloaded," and while watching the movie I heard " Emotions are designed to overwhelm logic and reasoning." Now I know it was just a movie, but to me those words were so true. Those words were true to me because time and time again I would find myself over and over again losing something logical because of my affected reasoning because of my emotions. It can move you or make you not want to move at all. Part 1 of "will" dealt with belief and Part 2 deals with passion, how it makes you feel.

So, yes express your feelings, but do it with the right people. Test them, make sure that they can hold water before you pour the gigantic vase of your dreams into them. I normally give it sometime and during that time I invite to places where others who love to take try to get them to talk. Again, passion is the key here it exposes and equips us to be more than what we are. When put to the test you will know one way or another. Remember you must have both parts of the will: "Belief" and "Passion," if you desire to go the distance from where you are and into your dreams. Say it with me, " I CAN, I KNOW I CAN , AND I WILL, AND I KNOW I WILL, I WILL DO IT!" Remember that the way you see things can and will, "Effects and affect how you experience" your moments.

Imagine if a word was a person, and that word had connected itself to another word by transfiguring that word and itself to make that possible.

The Word is "Don't," it's a simple and well known word. People know and use this word very often, and we just as words can choose to change. Imagine if "Don't" which means no access wanted to repent and change directions in its meaning and purpose in life, how would it make that change a reality? First, repeat after me, "I have to transfigure to transfigure!" You see we must become aware of a process to utilize that process on purpose and with a purpose. For the word "Don't" has taken away the core of the word "n_o_t" to become one with it, and what has been broken must become healed to transfigure the one back into two. "Don't" needs to become restored to "Do-not" before they can become the "Do" and the "Not" again. Now by restoring the "Not" the do can become free to be the "Do" and allow access!

Remember,

That Sight,

Brings with it,

<u>Awareness</u>!

So,

See Passionately!

CHAPTER 3
THE POWER OF ACTIONS

Have you ever heard of show me what you're workin with? Have you ever heard of the show me state? Do you believe what you saw a person doing more than what you hear them saying? The power of an action can make a believer out of just about anyone who sees it. Have you ever heard of seeing is believing?

Action + Spectators = Believers

When they see you doing it, then they will tell others what they saw. Actions produce, and people love fruit, especially fruit that they can see and taste because it equips them with the ability and nourishment to become more descriptive as they share what they saw. Yes, action creates storytellers and the greater the action the greater the story! Now, have you taken the time to consider what does it mean to be a spectator? Well just about all dictionaries will define it as a person who watches something somewhere. Are you a spectator, and do you watch yourself as well? Sounds wild huh, watching yourself while you're in the middle of doing something? This means that we have to become aware of our position, and how we move in that position. Some say you have to know where you are to know where you're going, others say you never know where you're going until you get there. It's even a song, "You never know where you're going until you get there!" What I am saying is that you have to have it, it meaning an understanding of your actions and what they represent. Again, what we do know is that people believe what they see, so if we can show our future in our present they can believe our future. I'll say it again;

"if we can show our future in our present, then they can believe our present will be in our future!"

In volume 1 of "Discover U," I share the importance of the acronym P.E.E.(Preparation, Experience and Evaluation), and how this system repositions your dreams from your mind into your moment. The way this is related to showing our future now, is hidden within "The Psychology of Preparation." **Preparation is setting things in order now for the future to come. When people see you preparing they know that you are expecting to do something or to go somewhere!** Remember actions speak louder than words!

Okay, our actions are like the paint brush which paints the images on the canvases of life for the believer to believe. Remember that most people say what they believe, and again actions are something that people believe. Most people say what they see! So, to paint with purpose, we must move with purpose, to ensure the painting in this case our actions are completely understandable in the minds of the spectators.

Well, we already know that actions speak louder than words, so do me a favor and say your desires as loud as you can, and what I mean by that, prepare for your dreams and live your dreams! Do it as often as possible and for as long as possible. Allow others around you to know that you mean business, and that you are more than just air and words. Show them that you are action!

What does action look like you might ask? I would respond, that it looks like:

- an answer for those who have a question,
- a solution for those who have problems, and
- service for those who desire to have a need met.

"Action is the Bridge between The Dreamer and The Dream."

Actions allow those around you to have a connection to the things that dwell within your heart and mind. Yes! Remember that Action is the required effort that bridges "The Dreamer" and "The Dream!" Actions bring "Intimacy!"

Intimacy is born from relationship, and relationship is conceived within actions. Most people still find themselves meeting to meet, but for me and most productive people around this world have meetings to activate movements. I say again;

"Meetings are to plan and <u>produce</u> Movements!"

"Hear me!" Is something we say in a meeting, "How was that?" Is something we say in a movement. A movement is anywhere we are willing to take action and move! What type of things cause you to move? Good question right? I know, I had to stop and make a list myself, because who should I take time to get to know more than myself? Are you important enough to yourself to take action for you? Now, now this is something that you can not answer with words alone, though that is part of the exercise to see if we are honest with ourselves. So, one part is to say, and the other part is to do!

Action takes place in your mind and within

your moment!

So, as we learned in kindergarten, as we show and tell we learn about others and they get a chance to learn about us. "Show and Tell" is even a song by Al Wilson, and when you hear it I hope it encourages you to smile too. Show being the mental and physical actions and tell being the verbal and written words. Make a list of things that you will do for yourself, and then write about how it felt to do those things for yourself. Remember actions speak louder than words, and a picture is worth a thousand words so take some pictures of you preparing for your dreams and living your dreams!

The Power of Actions are so vast, I could write for the rest of my life and never completely expose its power of influence, but I do my best to express its importance within this chapter. Have you ever heard of the phrase "Take Action?" If you did, you probably are saying to yourself that it means to do something and you are correct. I being me, tend to ask myself this question: "Does this have another meaning?" So, I would like to take you on the journey of:

"Does this have another meaning?"

"Take Action," and have you ever heard some say, " you should "Take Money" when you go to the store," and the answer is probably yes. You probably also heard someone say, "Take Help" if you are going to try to handle that! So, looking at "Take Action" from this vantage point equips us to see "Take Action" as something to bring along with us to utilize it at the proper time. As you can see the question changes the quest, which allows the change in choice, to change the challenge, because it changes what needs to be conquered!

I have a brief daily project that has altered my life in a major way which activates the two realities of "Take Action" that are presented above. The word OMEGA means end, and when people think of this word with action, they might think of end action. Now when you think of something in your mind that others might not have the capability to see on their own I call that a VISION.

I call this Project "OMEGA VISION" it is when you move with the end in mind. Yes, some call it goals, but for me goals are things to do, and "OMEGA VISION" is a way to see what you are doing which gives it purpose, and when I move with purpose, I move with passion. Passion for me brings discipline to my purpose, because I see correctly, I see it with "OMEGA VISION!" Yes, action with a purpose, and a purpose with a passion. Now to make this work I realized that every question must be answered with an "I Statement." Here is the question:

What does the end of my day look like?(Remember to answer with "I" statements) Set up categories, and say what the end outcome is for each day in that area.

Example:

What does the end of my day look like?

- Emotions-I managed my anger today,
- Family- I took time to talk to my child today,
- School- I finished my research for my paper,

- Fitness- I worked out for ½ hr today,
- Spiritual Life- I did what made God Joyful today.

OMEGA VISION is just a small way to insure that you "Take Action" and "Take Action" when it comes to preparing and living your dreams!

Remember,

That Action,

Brings with it,

Application!

So,

Be Persistent!

CHAPTER 4
THE TRIPLE "P" EFFECT

I know that there are many definitions of the word "Effect", and if there were time I could probably utilize them all. Right now I would like to focus on the verb usage form that is described on the Google search engine:

"Effect" cause (something) to happen; bring about.

You see before I describe the Triple P's I want you to be sure of what my purpose is for them, and I also want you to make my purpose your purpose!

Being that we are working on developing "OMEGA VISION" we should always move from here forward with the expected end in mind. Question, if you order a pizza and pay for it online, are you still expecting it to show up so that you can enjoy it? The effect of ordering and paying for the pizza should create an expectation of enjoying it right? I will respond for the both of us: "YES, of course if I paid for it, I want to eat it!" So, I would be correct in saying that doing something should "bring about" or "effect" an expected end. So, in the spirit of focusing on the end when starting I would like to say I will start with the last "P" first and the first "P" will be last, and the second will stay the second. Weird but true, huh, the middle stays the middle when you have 3 positions, and the first and the last switch. So, the Last "P" is "PERSISTENCE," which is described by the Google Search engine like this:

"PERSISTENCE" firm or obstinate continuance in a course of action in spite of difficulty or opposition.

To me that means that even when it's hard still hold on until the harvest! **<u>I tell myself all the time that "Persistence" requires "ACTION!"</u>** Now, as we combine these two wonderful words "Persistence" and "Effect" it should paint the picture that we should hold on until the end because we are expecting something to happen. Rewind back to the pizza, and imagine that we are really hungry! After ordering and paying for the pizza online we should strive to find the courage to endure the wait that might be caused by the lost or confused driver to enjoy the expected end of the delicious pizza. Can you remember a time when you utilized persistence and how it made you feel? If you are anything like me your response is: "Yes and No!" This is only due to the fact that sometimes greatness was at the end of the rainbow and other times garbage was! That's life, right? I have come to find out that we say that's life when you do not have an expected end in mind. So, to have "persistence" without the "effect" can create a rainbow without wonder. Hey, I am just working on creating happy endings on purpose and with a purpose.

So as we move in the mindset of the "Persistence Effect," it can create a higher level of motivation when you know the expected end. I know that I am better for this reality and I hope that the "Persistence Effect" will bring you as much drive as it has brought me to because

I understood and applied this part of the "Triple "P" Effect!"

The Middle or second "P" of the "Triple "P" Effect" is "PURPOSE!" Purpose is defined by the Google Search Engine this way:

"PURPOSE" the reason for which something is done or created or for which something exists.

For most people, they utilize this word to answer the great "Why am I here question," that mostly all people at one point in time tend to ask themselves. So, I will give you an example, "what might we say is a purpose of our lungs, one might respond, for breathing!" I know that my example might seem simple but it can be used to paint the understanding of this word in the mind of an 84 year old grandma and in the mind of her 4 year old great-granddaughter. You see there is no age limit on understanding purpose, whether you go up or down. So as before imagine if we connect the understanding of the words: "PURPOSE" and "EFFECT"; they would paint the picture of something being created for a reason with an expected end. **"PURPOSE" deals with sound because for me it determines how I hear what I hear!** Here is a simple but grabbable concept that brings that reality to life: "Toilet Paper!" When we think of what its purpose is and roll with it. I think that I allow "Toilet Paper" to fulfill its purpose at least twice a day. Imagine if I was about to do that for myself on purpose and with a purpose? I can, and so can you!

To activate the "PURPOSE EFFECT" as with any and all things we only need to understand and apply. As we have seen, and will now see on purpose, these concepts are necessary to be aware of to press beyond your position. We were created with a purpose and we also do things on purpose and as we couple what we do on purpose, with a purpose, our expected end becomes a dream that is transforming into a reality! So, we have been exposed to the reality of the "PERSISTENCE EFFECT" and the "PURPOSE EFFECT" two of the "Triple "P's" and how they both can impact the world as we know it as we choose to activate them. Remember a light cannot shine unless you flip the switch, and activate it by the power that is required for that light to shine. So, courageously flip that switch and become:

"A Change Agent!"

The third "P" of the "Triple "P" Effect" is "PASSION!" As you know I am utilizing the Google Search Engine to allow us to have the same platform to see the same vision to show that you can do what I am doing and "Live Your Dreams!" For me living your dreams is experiencing your passion! **<u>For me "PASSION"addresses my sight and how I see the world around me and within me.</u>** So, as we look at what the Google Search Engine shares it says:

"PASSION"

1) strong and barely controllable emotion.

2)The Suffering and death of Jesus.

That's a lot, but clearly a great way to engrave this word within our minds and hearts! When I think about "PASSION" I see it as beyond something that has driven me, I can feel it because it has pulled me! "PASSION" has pulled me through moments of brokenness to display my desire to love my wife the way God says she was created to be loved. I remember having a "PASSION" to graduate high school that pulled me through what my high school counselor said was impossible based on my past, but when my mother called her friend who was also a counselor she prepared a place for my "PASSION" to pull me through! Now, as before we will connect the concept of "PASSION and EFFECT" which exposes "HOW" the "PURPOSE" remains in a state of "PERSISTENCE" until it reaches it's expected end or what here we call the "EFFECT!"

The Triple "P" Effect can be more than a system that we know, it can if we choose become a strategy in the process of getting our dreams out of our head and into our moments.

As we activate and apply the "PERSISTENCE EFFECT", the "PURPOSE EFFECT" and the "PASSION EFFECT" we will see in our moments what others keep hidden in their minds. So when life feels heavy I would like to encourage you to consider applying the "Triple "P" Effect" to transport you from dreaming your dreams to living your dreams! Say it with me:

The **TRIPLE "P" EFFECT!**

It's the **"TRIPLE "P" EFFECT!**

WHAT?

I said

It's the **"TRIPLE "P"EFFECT!**

CHAPTER 5
SECOND TIME AROUND

Hindsight is 20/20 right? Most people say that when you look back on a situation you can always see what you could have done better; whether it be action or an ability that could have made the difference. We tend to think that what we know will make the difference in what we do, and for most that might be true. What if I were to say that I learned something different about the second time around, what some call hindsight, and that this information can change everything, but only if you are willing to trust it? It's like sitting in a chair made of paper, it could work if you're willing to trust it? Wow, trust is hard when you don't know the outcome or when you know the history of something. Trusting something that has not been battle tested for some might seem a bit strange, or maybe crazy as crazy. But trusting something and giving it a chance to be identified and placed in its proper position is what trust is all about. Even God when creating in the book of Genesis Chapter 1 took time to see and then separated things as they were identified and then placed them in their proper position.

Example/ Sample Genesis 1:1-5

"In the beginning God created the heavens and the earth. Now the earth was formless and empty, darkness was over the surface of the deep, and the Spirit of God was hovering over the waters. And God said, "Let there be light," and there was light. God saw that the light was good, and he separated the light from the darkness. God called the light "day" and the darkness he called "night." And there was evening, and there was morning--The First Day."(Bible, King James Version)

Imagine that, something has begun, a first day. I remember having a first day at school, at work, at college and most important in the relationships that matter most in my life. You see there for me must be "light," first as a presence, then as an example to show how and then an example to tell how. This is done to see who wants to become like the light, to hear and follow the process to come up out of the darkness and to become one with the light. You see, the fact of the matter is that we can believe something, and the only thing that it will change is our language, but when we decide to "TRUST" we become what we believe! We transform from being a

"DREAMER" into a "DOER!" You see a "DREAMER" considers all the possibilities, but a "DOER" conquers all the possibilities! Have you ever heard of a "Believe Fall Exercise?" Probably not, because getting others to believe some does not change their actions, but you have probably heard of a "Trust Fall Exercise!" Trust is something required to take action! Belief is a part of the awareness process, and is an important step in arriving at "TRUST!"

We dream about what we believe, but we do what we trust!

Just as in a dream, before we live it, we have to see it to be it! We have to be aware before we can achieve it! We have to believe it before we can build it! Again, we have to dream it before we can do it! Most people like me need things to come into their lives so that we see it to achieve it, and thus I have arrived at the phrase "Second Time Around!" As in the book of Genesis The Spirit hovered above the waters, displayed that it was in the room but not in the mess! Then it moved upon the face of the waters, where it addressed the void which was without form and showed it the form that it need to take to come out of the darkness, when God said, "let there be light!" Those that become aware and decided to achieve it, God saw, and divided them: the light from the darkness. God even gave them that Trust and obeyed him a name; "God called The Light "Day!""

Now those that were not aware and did not obey God

were Called: "Night!" You see when you have "Day" and "Night" you have to know when you're operating in the mindset of one or the other, because if you are like me you do not want to miss the second time around! So, to know when you are coming out of the "Day" and going into the "Night," it is called "Evening." "Evening," is when everything that is light begins to fade away and we move from hope to hopelessness. But, God has a different plan for us, so God speaks to us in darkness which is called "Night" and says let there be light!

You see, God desires for us to come out, so the light brings hope and then we began the mourning process. The mourning process is a desire to be in the light, which God called "Morning," which is coming out of the darkness into the light. Now, the process of evening and the morning gives birth to the "First Day," which to me exposes the process of "Belief" becoming "Trust!"

Seeing is believing, and believing comes from seeing, even if you are seeing it in a vision before you see it in your vision! Sometimes we show and other times we are shown. In others words sometimes we lead and other times we follow. First impressions make impact whether we want them to or not. Imagine if you had a cookout/party/barbeque at a park and a lot of people showed up. Everyone that shows up will not know you, but some will because it might be their second time around. Some will be in the light about who you are and others will be in the dark about who you are. Some will pay attention to your moves and what you say, and be concerned about what you heard and saw. These concerned people will create a divide that others can follow and choose not to follow. Now, those that respect you and did things to please you on purpose and that followed them you might notice, but those who choose to be rude and disrespect you, you will surely remember and make it a point to not allow them access to other things that are important to you. Let's for this chapter sake which focuses on second times around; you will call some "Day" whom you will want to deal with and the others "Night" that you would not want to deal with. Now, you might if you believe that access to them can benefit something in your life you might activate the "Evening" and "Morning" team to reposition those who are willing to change their situation. This is what God did in Genesis Chapter 1 verses 1 through 5.

We are made in God Image and likeness, which means we can look like God and Act like God.

Everything moves in a two step format; first step awareness, second step activation.

Example:

First Step: come into the room,

Second Step: connect with things within the room.

Awareness can be conscious or unconscious, but be assured that awareness is a must in step one. Understanding your reality is a must when establishing awareness. Remember that the Bible says in 2nd

Chronicles chapter 20 verse 20 that: *"Believe in The Lord your God, so shall ye be established; believe in his prophets, so shall ye prosper."*

Example:

First Step (Awareness): come into the room, (Believe in The Lord your God, so shall ye be established)

Second Step(Activation): connect with things within the room, (Believe in his prophets, so shall ye prosper)

Just as in Genesis, we must become aware of the light and its value before we can truly trust and be true to our destiny. God, just as the light, comes into our situation to take us to a destination to fulfill our destiny.

Everyone has a different second time around at different times in their lives, and the way we handle them will determine how we process our past, experience or present and prepare for our future.

Remember the flashlight and the laser-beam concepts in chapter 1? Step one is like the flashlight because it brings things to your awareness, and step 2 is like the laser-beam because it allows you to cut through opposition to arrive at your desired location. Even though it seems different it's connected if we reach-out and see how the concepts connect by focusing on how they move.

Now let's step outside of your comfort zone and

add a little more to Step1 and step 2 process by focusing on two words that you have heard of called "Systems" and "Strategies!"

Systems V's Strategies

Have you ever heard of the Do's and the Don't? Have you ever heard of the Movers and the Shakers? Have you ever heard of the Thinkers and the Doers?

<u>Well to be clear and to the point I will say it like this:</u>

-Systems- "Are ways <u>TO</u> do things," and

-Strategies- "Are ways <u>YOU</u> do things!"

The difference maker is the "To" and the "You," get it? To you, it's up "TO" "YOU!"

I know right, it's like a secret message, you see

the system is pointing towards something "to" make something happen, and the strategies are showing us who that someone is, to make something happen! Systems point, and strategies require play to bring the concepts to life. My goal is to equip you and remind you that a thought expressed in your mind is one thing and a thought expressed in your moment is something totally different, it's the difference between saying: systems and strategies! It's the difference between "Dreamers" and "Doers!"

    Imagine you walk into a dance hall, and you saw a person that was doing all the right things and moving in all the right ways. This is what I call step1, because now you are aware and have eyes to see and you are looking. I know for me, when I see something that desire to the point of wanting to experience beyond my dreaming, I begin to bring step2 to life. I go from hope to faith real fast, and I find myself craving what's in my mind to exist in my moment. I go from can and could to should and how do I, do you know anyone who can help me make this possible! I need to know how to dance real good real fast or at least bust some moves that will gain the attention that I am look for!

Everything is always done with a purpose, and I say with expectations, because when you know what's in it for you, it positions you to be more in it! Get it, if you do not now, when you do get it, you will get it.

Have you ever heard of the statement, " Get the Mind and the body will follow,"and for me as I evaluated my past this has been true for me, has it been for you? If you have ever been in a car with a rearview mirror, you know that I is designed to allow you to see backwards while looking forward. WOW! Imagine that, being able to look back while your focus is in front of you. So, in "Discover U Part 1, chapter 2," I was sharing about the dynamic of connecting to what you want and how to ensure its success by creating the winning team system, which I learned from Dr. Myles Munroe, and Delatorro McNeal II, whom to me are heros living the dream I am manifesting. Both, understand the power of having support in the areas that make all the difference when it comes to living your dreams verses dying with your dreams. Some people are great at keeping secrets, and they know how to take them to the grave. Now, the sad thing about that is the fact that some people keep their dreams as a secret, and take their dreams to the grave, and thus making the grave the richest place on the planet. I am refusing to sow my dreams in the grave, and I am asking you to do the same, so do more than just dream your dreams and experience your dreams.

    I have found myself sad, discouraged and mad, because of lack of action. These feelings have come and come again when I do not activate the principle concept expressed in this chapter, which is "Trust!" When you trust you can have more than action, it can give you peace. I would like to warn and encourage you that peace is more than a product of trust, it is something for me more than what I have and am continuing to understand. Peace is a knowing that things are in the best hands, and that you have done all that you can do and that you are trusting someone and something that is the Most reliable things in all of existence, Love! Now, I am not talking about the kind of love that we have come to know in this reality, or the kind that we think we are looking for and try to share. I am speaking of the love that is beyond our comprehension, one that breaks you down and builds up that's hard to put in words, that type of love. A love that is so beyond us we have to allow it to speak of itself, but not by what it says but by what others cannot say about it! It's this unspeakable awe that everything and everyone knows of and finds it hard to believe, and yet somehow we trust it when we are down to nothing because we trust it is up to everything that can get it done when we can or cannot! How do you trust something with no limits and no boundaries the first time around? Great question right? Well for me at first it usually happened the second time around, and thus the name of this chapter the second time around.

You see, for most when they are aware of the value of something, whether it be because of what someone perform or present. Have you ever thought of those two words, "PERFORM" and "PRESENT?" "Perform", just as step 1 deals with doing something to obtain awareness by doing something, and "Present" just as step2 is offering an opportunity to connect to something that will make you greater to get through your challenge.

Here is something that is wild to me but it's true.

John chapter 6 verses 45 and 46:

(45)"It is written in the prophets, and they shall be all taught of God. Every man therefore that hath heard, and hath learned of the Father, cometh unto me.

(46) Not that any man hath seen the Father, save he which is of God, he hath seen the Father."

These two verses through The Holy Spirit has revealed a revelation to me that has altered my vision and sight. For we all know that real knowledge is to protect or to produce for someone or something we love. Ever heard of the passion of the Christ? It changed how He saw what we saw happening to him, which is as an opportunity not as an oppression.

Example:

Step1: "1 John 4:8; He that loveth not knoweth not God; for God is love," Love came and brought the hope of something that we can trust in to become one with that love. So we will call "Love" here the Father, because Love will hover above us and show us a hope of peace in our situation and say "Let there be light." In a way saying I will sent my offspring to show you how to be in my image and likeness.

Step2: "Ephesians 2:13-16;"

(13)But now in Christ Jesus ye who sometimes were far off are made nigh by the blood of Christ."

(14) For he is our peace, who hath made both one, and hath broken down the middle wall of partition between us;

(15)Having abolished in his flesh the enmity, even the law of commandments contained in ordinances; for to make in himself of twain one new man, so making peace;

(16) And that he might reconcile both unto God in one body by the cross, having slain the enmity thereby:

(17)And came and preached peace to you which were afar off, and to them that were nigh."

As we can see Jesus Christ became our "Peace," and if only the son can see the Father, then it must also be true that only "Peace" can See "Love." So, if we apply this to Genesis chapter 1 verses 1 through 5 as applied in this book "Love" came to prepare a place for "Peace." You see "Love" is the only thing that can move in the darkness without being affected by the darkness. "Love" did this to bring us out of darkness into the light by bringing us back into "Love," but this time not just for Love to hover over us to for "Love" to be one with us by us becoming one with "Peace."

Chapter 6
A Higher Vibration

Sound vibrates, and as it does so it gives our actions something to align with, which can take us higher or lower, so to ensure that we can become living words! Imagine become something that most can only dream of, which for some is identifying the limits and then taking the limits off. Imagine placing yourself in a wall just to knock those walls down, because sometimes we have to box ourselves in to shine beyond the limits of those walls. To me a wall is a place we build to get our thoughts together. So, be encouraged to become brighter than your strength and resources will allow you to be, by connecting with those who can equip us to be beyond the time and space of the box that we have boxed ourselves in. Have you ever heard of a frequency? As "Andre 3000" from the Music Group "Outcast" says in his song, "Vibrate Higher!" A frequency to me is something that you can tune into, so my question to you is what frequencies have you tuned into? Have you ever found yourself being a frequency for others to tune into? Have you taken them higher or lower when they tuned into you? Did you go higher or lower when you tune or tuned into others? In moments we offer and receive offerings, it's like a handshake sometimes we extend a hand for others to receive and other times we make the choice to receive or deny the hands that are extended to us. Either we tune into the frequency offered or deny it.

To tune into the frequency is to make a choice is to choose to vibrate in harmony, and to deny the frequency is to chose to be off key. Sometimes it's okay to harmonize and other times its okay to be off key, we just have to have the courage to find peace in the choices that we make. Choices like these are the choices that make legendary leaders and they also make legendary losers!

Learning How to Dreamwalk

If we think that "Hurt" is only physical, we might have never heard of a hurt heart? Can something emotional also be physical? The phrase: "as a man thinks so is he" is True for me! Is it for you? It is more than a phrase it is a scripture from the Bible in the Book of

Proverbs 23 verse 7; which reads "For as he thinketh in his heart, so is he: Eat and drink, saith he to thee; but his heart is not with thee." This has taught me that when my heart, mouth and moves are not united it affects everything around me. I'll tell you, I've been up and felt like the sun rising in the morning, coming up out of all my mess. I mean I have found myself feeling so good moving towards feeling so great. Have you ever saw something and as you moved towards it, everything just felt right? It's an indescribable feeling of belonging that's hard to wrap words around, even though we always try to. I have been so up, and felt like everything that was down was so far down that eyes could not perceive and mind could not conceive what was thriving and surviving in the belly of hurt. You know when some get a chance to dream they dream of something small like a peanut, when I dream I like to dream of the peanut factory and the peanut fields. Can you say, "Take the limits off?" Can you say, "Take the gimmicks off?" I find myself asking, "how far can this go, and am I being pushed or pulled to connect with this dream?" I remember reading a book written by T.D. Jakes called "Great Questions" and I learned that great questions produce great solutions. It's one thing to have the power to overcome, and a whole different thing to utilize something. To have something is to posse, and to utilize something is to produce. Step 1 posses, and step 2 produce; God said, "If you take one step I will take 2" is revealed in the themes across the whole bible to me.

Example:

This scripture will be broken down into three parts.

2 Chronicles 20:20 (KJV)

Part 1; Our Step 1 (they got into position to hear from The Lord)

20(A) *And they rose early in the morning, and went forth into the wilderness of Tekoa: and as they went forth, Jehoshaphat stood and said, Hear me, O Judah, and ye inhabitants of Jerusalem:* (Just as they got into position to hear from the Lord we need to also get into position to hear from The Lord as well. People can not obey what they cannot hear, but we can obey what we hear so be encouraged to get into position to hear from the Lord.)

Part 2; God's Step 1

20(B) *Believe in the Lord your God, so shall ye be established;* (This is where God begins by doing a work within you, changing your heart and your mind; in turn changing your desires and perspectives!)

Part 3; God's Step 2

20(C) *Believe His prophets, so shall ye prosper.* (This is where God sends others to share their seed-times and harvests of obeying and applying the Word of the Lord! Now as you remember that The Lord is not a respecter of persons rather a respecter of principles, and as Dr. Mike Murdock teaches: we attract what we respect. Now if The Lord is a respecter of principles then The Lord is looking to attract principles!)

Proverbs 4:7 says,

"Wisdom is the principal thing; therefore get wisdom: and with all thy getting get understanding."

This means that The Lord is looking for wisdom, and not just any wisdom but the wisdom that comes from Him! Now, from that it stresses "with all thy getting get understanding," which means that understanding is something that will make all the difference. As seen in the bible in book of Proverbs 2:6 exposes what The Lord gives, and what comes from His mouth, so I will let you read it for yourself so that you can say exactly what I said when I read it, "WOW, this is what dreamwalking is all about!"

Proverbs 2:6 says,

"For The Lord giveth <u>wisdom</u>; from His mouth

comes <u>knowledge</u> and <u>understanding</u>."

It does not get any clearer than that, it shows what The Lord gives and what comes from His mouth, so my question is; are we receiving and listening? Are we fools?

Proverbs 1:7 says,

"The fear of LORD is the is the beginning of knowledge; but fools despise wisdom and instruction."

So, I ask the question when have despised The Lord's wisdom and instruction and not feared The LORD and operated as a fool? I know, why should I fear any man? Well, after thinking about that for a while I realized that The LORD is not a man, and that changed everything! Fearing The LORD is the beginning of things that will transform my: mind, body and spirit. As shared in

Proverbs 1:7 it is the beginning of Knowledge, and as we read:

Proverbs 9:10 which says,

"The fear of The LORD is the beginning of Wisdom: and The Knowledge of the Holy One is Understanding."

Now, from Proverbs 9:10 we see that wisdom that fools despise that The LORD gives exposes a special type of Knowledge. This Knowledge is Knowledge of The Holy One, which is what The LORD has labeled as "Understanding," as stated in Proverbs 9:10. So, when you read about what I call dreamwalking in this scripture,

Proverbs 4:7 says,

"Wisdom is the principal thing; therefore get wisdom: and with all thy getting get

understanding."

Know that The LORD is doing this to lead us to knowledge of HIM! His knowledge leads to HIM! When The LORD gives us wisdom He gives us HIM! The LORD is the principal thing, He is the understanding that we should get in all thy getting!

STEP 1:

Receive the wisdom that The LORD gives, Proverbs 2:6 and focus of the Knowledge and understanding that comes from His mouth!

STEP 2:

Make it a point to allow the Wisdom to lead you to Knowledge of The Holy One, which is what The LORD calls Understanding! Bring back to The LORD what He gives you to arrive at Understanding. This will ensure that you learn and apply DreamWalking in an unstoppable way on your second time around!

I knew it!

Have you ever thought something that you hoped wasn't true but later you came to find out that your deepest fears were actualized and said, "I knew it?" Have you ever been surprised by your deepest desires, to the point of tears falling off your face drenching your shirt and said, "I knew it?" Well, I've been there, and I'll tell you it was bad when it was bad but when it was good it was great and said, "I knew it!" Hope, it can feed you things that can equip you with a strength that can take you through anything, and when you get there you will say, "I knew it!" On the other hand, Hopelessness can drain you in a way that will make everything impossible, and you will say, "I knew it!" Have you ever heard of that song that says, "A Penny for your thoughts, a nickel for a kiss and a dime if you tell me that you love me." I like to call it the 16 cents of a relationship. In this book many platforms of perspectives will be exposed to enlighten and empower the readers to relate to others that they might engage as they live life and develop relationships that will mold, mess-up and manipulate how they perceive.

I once heard a preacher's son named Kyle Rodgers sang in one of his songs that, "Life is what you make it, so make something of yourself, put those guns down and take those books off the shelf!" I challenged me to evaluate why I went to war, and what had me fighting in the first place. Now, those questions birth this concept:

Theme:

It's A Fight:

- Focus-1: Who's in the ring?
- Focus-2: Who's winning?
- Focus-3: Who do I want to win?

Focus-1: Who's in the Ring?

Why do I have these weapons in my hands and greater weapons on the shelf while I am in this ring? What! You are probably asking what do this man mean about having greater weapons on the shelf, and I will once again respond with a resounding yes, I got greater ones on the shelf! Have you ever heard of the concept that the pen is mightier than the sword?

Why is the pen mightier than the sword? Well, first of all it can leave words that stay. Words that stay can become a way of life, and they can also become what we know as the law, all because the "PEN!" Learning to make goals with that "PEN" is what I am learning to do in this ring as I fight to get to knock those goals down. Get it, it's going down, those goals going down! So, who's in the ring:

    you,

    your pen, and

    your goals!

Knowing this has made a major impact on my daily efforts to manifest my goals within my moments. So knowing who's in the ring because it can and will make the difference if we allow it to. **So, as we look in the ring we see:**

- **Ourselves,**
- **Opponents, and**
- **The Referee's.**

If we can see ourselves in the ring and understand our role we can truly understand what is being expected from us. "What do I look like in this situation," is something that I learned that I must ask myself. When they see me do they seen my Father, because Christ said that when you see me you see the father and The Father is

"LOVE!" Do I display Love? in the bible in the book of 1st Corinthians chapter 13 displays the images of Love; in us, around us, on us and through us. Be reminded that Love in action is being described as Charity.

1st Corinthians Chapter 13:1-13

Verse (1)

"Though I speak with the tongues of men and of angels, and have not charity (love), I am become as sounding brass, or a tinkling cymbal."

In verse (1) 1st Corinthians Chapter 13 exposes the power behind the language of love from the Divine Prospective. Here it exposes for us to understand that language without love will *"become as a sounding brass, or a tinkling cymbal."* Imagine that, words need to have an expectation connected to them. If I say "it's time to eat" the people that hear me should prepare to eat something. I see it as this **"empty words are just letters that are only making a sound without a purpose."**

Verse (2)

"An though I have the gift of prophecy, and understand all mysteries, and have all knowledge; and though I have all faith, so that I could remove mountains, and have not charity (LOVE) I am nothing."

In verse (2) of 1st Corinthians Chapter 13 exposes the power behind the gift, and what the end of that gift is. Imagine having all faith so that you can remove mountains, and yet being seen as nothing. Imagine being able to solve every mystery and yet you are not being booked as an investigator. **It's like being the most valuable poorman on the planet, because all that you produce is perceived as valueless.** It shows that the values in the gifts comes from "Charity(Love)." **God is the giver of all gifts that are good and perfect, and I like to say Christ brings the value to the vinared!**

Verse (3)

"And though I bestow all my goods to feed the poor, and though I give my body to be burned, and have not charity, I am nothing."

In verse (3) 1st Corinthians Chapter 13 exposes the power behind bestowing all, and giving your body once again is Charity(Love). **To bestow is more than just having a gift, it is actually utilizing that gift in a surprising way to transform someone's life by**

ensuring that they connect with what that gift produces. Even if a person produce what should be conceived, perceived and received as valuable, they won't engage it correctly because of the lack of love(Charity).

Verses (4-8)

"(4) Charity suffereth long, and is kind; charity envieth not; charity vaunteth not itself, is not puffed up,

(5) Doth not behave itself unseemly, seeketh not her own, is not easily provoked, thinketh no evil;

(6) Rejoiceth not in iniquity, but rejoiceth in the truth;

(7) Beareth all things, Believeth all things, hopeth all things, endureth all things.

(8) Charity never faileth: but whether there be prophecies, they shall fail; whether there be tongues, they shall cease; whether there be knowledge, it shall vanish away."

In verses (4-8) 1st Corinthians Chapter 13 exposes the power concealed within "Charity(LOVE)." So let's take a closer look as how Charity is revealed within the situations expressed verse by verse.

(Situation 1)
Verse (4a)

Charity suffereth long, and is kind;

"How do you suffer long and be kind?" is a great question to start off with to expose the power hidden within the Charity. I remember suffering and I know that it took the power of God to assist me to love on those that were causing the frustration and pain that I was feeling. I knew that on my own I would have found my hand trying to stop the pain. Have you ever heard of the left and right sleeping pill? I'm joking but on the flip side

I'm not because sometimes, people in life will take you there. Now, when people take me there to a place that I know that wont please God Most High I need the Holy Spirit that was sent by Christ to assist me to bring the Word of God to life by leading and guiding me to be kind. You see it's a difference between getting mad and getting angry, and knowing the difference between the two will make the difference. When suffering long most tend to get mad, which explains why most lose it when they get mad. On the other hand being angry can allow you to suffer long while being kind through love which will release "righteous indignation" instead of being mad and producing "rage."

Situation (2)

Verse (4b)

charity envieth not;

I am Jealous, is something that charity will never say because charity is there to sow and cultivate the harvest. Ever been eager before, you know, to get something that you want with a bubbling deep burning desire? Well, that's kind of like what it's like to envy. To want something so bad until you get so mad, but when someone who loves in action and brings charity into your circumstances. You see, being eager without being enlightened with the power of charity doesn't equip you with the wisdom and peace which surpasses all understanding. Now, on the other hand when charity is is the mix, exchanging, sowing and reaping become apart the equation. **Know this:**

- **Their is a difference between:**
  - **Giving and Sowing,**
  - **Taking and Receiving,**

understanding the differences allows you to see the difference and applying the differences allows you to experience the differences!

What's the difference between "Giving and Sowing?" you might be asking yourself, and I will say to you, "That's a great question!" Giving represents offering someone something, which might or might not be activated or received by that person.

Examples:

- Give me a chance(Opportunity),
- Give me something to drink(Hydration),
- Give me something to eat(Nurishment),
- Give me your attention(Support),
- Give me a hand (Power/Strength),
- Give me undivided attention(A Platform)

This is something that is paramount to know when you are in the "Ring," because knowing who you are can make the difference in how you fight and what your fighting for when you are in the ring with other things and other people. Self awareness positions us to become located and repositioned, thus activating the biblical concept of "Going from Faith to Faith and from Glory to Glory." If we can see who is our opponents we can truly see our problems as an opportunity because we can address them as a situation and not a problem. If we can find a way to see the referee's perspectives, we will become equipped to become informed of the rules and guidelines by perceiving life from a situational perspective.

Focus-2: Who's Winning?

Most of the days I found myself fighting a losing battle as I tried to make everyone happy, instead of trying to assist everyone in manifesting their dreams and that's where I went wrong. I read something in the bible that helped me to gain a greater understanding of this concept of who's winning and it was broken up into three parts with the same phrase which is this:

- **"you will be measured according to the measure which you mete withal."**

There are three ways that I have learned to mete withal:

-Hear, (Mark 4:24)

-Judge, (Matthew 7:1)

-Give, (Luke 6:38)

Let's take a closer look at how the way we hear, judge and give plays a major role in **"Understanding"** and **"Equipping"** who will win in the ring.

So, how does hearing play a role in understanding who will win in the ring? In the King James Bible in the book of Mark, chapter 4 verse 24, exposes the power in how we hear and how others hear us.

Mark 4:24

"And He said unto them, Take heed what ye hear: <u>with what measure ye mete, it shall be measured to you:</u> and unto you that hear shall more be given."

Understanding can be seen as many things, but for me I choose to utilize the King James Bible book of Proverbs Chapter 9 verse 10 definition which says "The fear of the Lord is the beginning of wisdom: and knowledge of the Holy One is Understanding." Knowledge of the Holy One, what a way to describe understanding. I have learned that what you hear with your ear is one thing, and how you hear with your ear is a totally different thing. Now for me understanding has been a key, when it came to crossing the bridge from the perspective of knowledge to perspective of wisdom. I realized that to hear information without understanding restricted my perspective of knowledge, and that was good for good conversation. Now, when I found myself wanting to do more than just talk, understanding became more valuable than anything else that I possessed, because I desired to arrive within the perspective of wisdom and for this I needed to cross the bridge of understanding. How do I take heed of what and how I hear, has been the question for me. It lead me to the question "What perspective am I listing from:

- A Knowledge Perspective? or
- A Wisdom Perspective?

If it's one of knowledge that I might get stuck as a dreamer, and that might be more than most because most never have the courage to dream. **Now on the other hand if it's one of wisdom, then I might get caught being a doer!**
Now for me that's something to be speechless about, because actions speak louder than words! So, I will utilize wisdom to allow my actions to speak for me.

Matthew 7:1-2

"Judge not, that ye be not judged. For with what judgment ye judge, ye shall be judged: *and with what measure ye mete, it shall be measured to you again.*"

The power Judgement or of the decision, not only affect the we engage those around us, it also engages how we see ourselves. Now, we can seek to find ourselves within ourselves, or we can be greater and search to find Christ within us first and understand that we are made in his image to look like him, and we can also find ourselves moving like Christ who is addressing what we activate the character of christ. I use to think that I attracted the opposite, but in reality I attracted those that were like me. Those that moved like me, walked like me and talked like me, I realized that I was looking for myself and Christ is doing the same thing. Being that everything was made through Christ by Christ and for Christ, whenever Christ agrees with Himself whoever agrees with Christ wins. This concept brings Galatians 2:20 to life for me.

Galatians 2:20 KJV

"I am crucified with Christ: nevertheless I live; yet not I, but Christ liveth in me: and the life which I now live in the flesh I live by the faith of the Son of God, who loved me, and gave himself for me."

So, I now have a greater understanding that it is victory within Christ, whether it's me in Christ or Christ in me! No matter how it goes judging whether Christ is in position and also determining how to get Christ in position will make all the difference for me. Christ can be utilized as the Supreme Judge and process of Judgment for Christ's Judgment has brought mankind into a position of judging righteously with a focus on pleasing The Father Whom has bared witness of who Christ is to Him, and said in:

- Matthew 3:17 KJV

"And lo a voice from heaven, saying, This is my beloved Son, in whom I am well pleased.",

- Matthew 17:5 KJV

"While he yet spake, behold, a bright cloud overshadowed them: and behold a voice out of a cloud, which said, This is my Beloved Son, in whom I am well pleased; hear ye him.",

- John 12:28 KJV
"Father, glorify thy name. Then came there a voice from heaven, saying I have both glorified it, and will glorify it again."

I would like to note that when you move in such a way that The Father from heaven releases a voice from heaven to bear witness of who you are and what you are doing it is important to me to pay attention, and I hope you might be considering the same.

Luke 6:38

Give, and it shall be given unto you; good measure, pressed down, and shaken together, and running over, shall men give into your bosom. <u>For with the same measure that ye mete withal it shall be measured to you again.</u>

To give, is a very tricky thing, because you must find someone who is ready to receive. To release we must find someone to receive, it's like playing catch with someone verses playing catch with yourself. If you (1) hear right and (2) judge right but have challenges with

(3)give to someone who <u>desires to receive</u> and <u>know how to receive,</u> then and only then can you receive a harvest. Having a desire and know how makes all the difference when it comes to seedtime and harvest, or getting a return on what you give. **"A Desire" is wanting something in a intense way, verse's "A Know how" which is understanding of how to bring that desire to life or how to connect the knowledge with the understanding.**

Having a measure to mete something with the expectation that the same effort that you release will become a standard that will become the process. Another way of understanding this is the system that becomes the strategy, which transform your situation and connects you with solutions. Again, be reminded that Christ gave in such a way, that everyone that Christ gave to had their lives impacted and changed in a major way.

Focus-3: Who do I want to Win?

To say it plainly, I want to win! Now, remembering that the fight is fixed, will assist me in deciding who I want to win; For Christ is King of Kings and Lord of Lords. He is the boss of bosses, and all must answer to Christ. So, I realized that I can want me or someone or something to win all day, but at the end of the movie Christ always wins before the credits roll. So, I am learning to want what God wants and I have been blessed with a system to assist me in doing just that which is derived from Luke 12:12.

Luke 12:12 KJV

"For the Holy Ghost shall teach you in the same hour what ye ought to say."

You see, I have come to learn that The Holy Ghost has already been equipped with what the Lord God said about me before the world begun, so by plugging into the Holy Ghost it teaches me how to prophecy the perspective of God Most High. The Lord made a way within His Holy Ghost for it contains The Grace of God Most, and when it becomes our Truth that the fullness of who Christ is will be revealed when our actions and words say, "come Lord!"

Poem Expression:

40 Days
"For These Days"

Moses go back to Egypt and show the deliverance,
allowing chains to bounce off the ground.

What we do at work we should teach and do at home!
This brings strength to the dome, teaching our offspring how to rome.
steps are like cycles that spin us off on a path:

Step 1 get out of basket what you needed to work, and watch those haters turn into jerks.

Step 2 wash by hand in tub and scrub and rinse, remember life is beyond the intense.

Step 3 hang up, vibrate in a realm above and pay attention to the Spirit of Love.

Step 4 take down and iron, get prepared to grind and work the vision that you found in your mind.

Step 5 fold and put away, and then it's time to play because your goal was achieved for the day.

Remembers boundaries; are a key to success, and people around you celebrate your success. and your gift without love is a verses people plot in their minds not something that their seeking to find.

Remind the that you see when you look in the mirror, that the Lord blesses whatever you put your hands too, just like He Did for Jesus, we are His temple and He don't ever want to leave us.

Know this:
There is a difference between taking someone somewhere and moving someone somewhere?
the take is a visit, and the move is a remain!

Genesis 11 exposes a perspective that takes us
Up in His name, and Out into fame,
up the tower, and out of the city!

Game On, Game Up I pray that you hear me!
Game Out!

7 CHAPTER
TRANSFORMING TRANSMISSIONS

Knowing what you release, and releasing what you know can make all the difference. There is a **"Thief"** that is out to <u>"take"</u> your perspective and make it one of a lessor one, and there is a **"Chief"** that is out to <u>"transform"</u> your perspective to make it a greater one. Both the Thief and the Chief have a mission to impact your **"Transmissions!"** .What we release determines what we receive, again: the type of seed determines the type of harvest. Everything has an assignment. The "Thief's" job is to take your valuables with or without you knowing. The "Chief's" job is to increase your valuables with or without you knowing.

The Thief:

{John 10:10

(10) The thief cometh not, but for <u>to steal</u>, and <u>to kill</u>, and <u>to destroy</u>: I am come that they might have life, and that they might have it more abundantly.}

The purpose of the Thief is clearly defined as: to steal, to kill and to destroy. This to me is a warning to identify when I allow a thief in my life to influence me, and it also exposes the agenda of the thief. As I focus on the actions, perspectives and communication of the thief I can increase my level of effectiveness when engaging the thief that come into my life to equip them with the right things to steal as I present the fruits of the spirit as described is Galatians chapter 5 verses 22 through 23. Doing this with the intent to transform their transmission from working their will to working the will of the one who sent me.

The Chief:

Matthew 20:25-28

{ 25But Jesus called them *unto him*, and said, Ye know that the princes of the Gentiles exercise dominion over them, and they that are great exercise authority upon them. 26But it shall not be so among you: but whosoever will be great among you, let him be your minister; 27And whosoever will be chief among you, let him be your servant: 28Even as the Son of man came not

to be ministered unto, but to minister, and to give his life a ransom for many.}

As revealed here, the Chief; should be the servant of all who follow them. In other words; we would do well to keep the trees in our garden, for the fruit of their production is our harvest. This is true whether we are a Chief or a Thief, but the Chief does this for the glory of the Lord, which in turn will bring you what I like to call "The Oil of Joy!"

Doing this allows us to give our lives as a ransom for as many as has the courage to come into the atmosphere that we dwell in. For greater is he that is within us than he who is with the world. In other words the Spirit Man is greater than the Flesh Man. I say it another way, your inner man is greater than your outer man. Now even though one is greater than the other together, if they move in unity nothing shall be impossible for us. It is the fullness of what a united mind and body looks like because they are being spirit lead. Now, there are many spirits but there is only one Most High Spirit, whichever spirit you choose to be lead by is up to you. Be reminded that Some spirits have been designed to move as "The Thief" or "The Chief," whichever one you submit to and support will be the one that will rule and reign in your life.

This chapter is not long in writing, for it is designed for you to think over and plunder for a long time. Some thoughts can be done: with passions, with words and with actions! All are equally important, so "Take Time" just as we have been encouraged to "Take Action!"

CHAPTER 8
WALKING IN PERFECTION

The wit "Peace."

<u>POEM</u>
BY ME, DEDERICK D. WOODARD
"STUMBLING AND FALLING FOR THE RIGHT THINGS"

When you stumble, fall for the right things,

Get ready for the least to trip up the game and to become the greatest,

Moving for an encounter with The Lord will qualify you for Upgrade and a higher level of clearance to have a higher level of clarity,

This is your hour, so remember what you do will do you, so Do the Almighty, so that the Almighty can do you, and

And victory will be experienced because of one simple thing, God: was, is and will be on our side, and

If God is for you whom is in the Cornerstone that we should find in us and us in it, we should pray for instructions on how to properly come out fighting with our hands up, and

Remembering that purpose is something that we can stumble upon, but to do that we must come out of the corner allowing the cornerstone to guide our path, and

To become the right person at the right place at the right time engaging with the right person, and

Know that as a man I can make my plans, but also remembering that The Lord is my Navigator who instructs me when to move, where to move and how to move, and

Knowing that at the end of the day there are two types

of plans a man can plan to plan; to activate my will or the Will of The Lord, and

Falling in right place, with the right face, doing the right things, is the fullness of the gift making room for the giver, and

Being in the place that has not yet fully become the place for the situation has not yet made a demand for the solution, and

Sensing in your spirit that you are close to that moment in time and space, but stumbling to collect the words to express the concept in your communication with others, and

Knowing in you "knower" that you are too close to allow anything to prevent you from reaching your breakthrough, and

Realizing that you are in the right field stumbling to connect with the right spot, and

You find yourself racing your racing heart rate, and as the pressure is building inside you and around you, you find yourself rejoicing because of what you're expecting to happen, and

Excitement flows through your body as blood flows your veins experiencing the fullness of the journey which is over 60,000 miles in distance which could take you around the world more than twice, and

Being mindful to survive until you stumble across prosperity because I was in the field of my dreams collecting what fruit I could identify, and

Doing all that I could to encourage myself because I was down to nothing and whenever I am down to nothing The Lord is always up to something, and

Not knowing the details but knowing the destination I was assured that something was about to happen, and

Knowing that from God's Point of View nothing just happens, which is a perspective from heaven to earth, but as a man seeing from a man's perspective not knowing the plans of The Lord but planning to move when the Lord commands I often appear as if I always one way or another somehow find myself stumbling and falling for the right things, and

Realizing that I was where I was not because I was so sure of myself, but rather because I was so sure of The Lord, and

Realizing that I did not have detail, but what I did have was determination, and

Arriving in a place of abundance unaware and surprised, as The Lord showed and shared with me level by level to bringing me closer and closer into His Presence and Prospective, and

Weeping and Worshiping, crying out to The Lord and asking The Lord to get involved in my mind and my moments, and

Realizing that without the mind of Christ as a christian I am only a second rate citizen in a first class society, and

Being in the place and assisting with producing the product but not being apart of the team, left me with an empty void just as you find the earth in the book of Genesis before God said, "Let there be light, and there was light," and

I am a man, and Christ is the Light of Man and without him in my life I cannot comprehend Him whom is called Christ, and

Without Christ I cannot find the blessing within the but whooping and God Chastise those that He loves, and God so loved the world that He gave His only Begotten Son to correct our performance, and

This is the power to activate the shift that we have been desiring for as long as we have been dreaming, and

When even we ourselves find ourselves saying no way in the world could it be possible, we learn to correct our speech and say I can do all things through Christ who strengthens me, and

Every now and then when we feel a little weak The Lord orders another step out of His righteous servants, because in our weakness His power is made perfect and

Just as in the beginning when God created the heaven and the earth he had to let there be some things to make it possible for what needs to be formed to become formed, and

As we stumble from being formed to being made The Lords is able to create in us a clean heart, and

Realizing that I and you both know that I do deserve this position on my own merit, but because God said Let there be light, and I stumbled on that place called there and found that light and allowed it to give me the power to become the Sons of God I now can do as my Father do, and

I too can leave bread crumbs as well to trip others into the stability of the power of God, and they may also say I am stumbling to fall for the right things!

I am going to stumble blind, and trusting The Lord to become my sight!

I am going to stumble and press until I am positioned!

I am going to stumble and do what I got to do to get into the right place, where there is a right time and a right season!

I am going to stumble in the corner of my dream until The Lord call me out of the Corner of the Field of my dreams!

I find myself finding handfuls of fruit on purpose, that are unnatural to the natural as breadcrumbs trail to encourage me to just keep coming!

I am bundling the things that The Lord is instructing me to bundle to reap the harvest of the Earth!

I also am allowing Christ to equip me to speak the things of Heaven to bind them on Earth as they are bound in Heaven, thus creating a harvest in Heaven and in Earth as I bundle what The Lord has bundled!

I am about my Father's business as My Lord The Lord: was, is and will be about the Father's business, and as The Lord has bundled His harvest in Heaven I will bundle His harvest in the Earth even if I must stumble along the way, for His is The Way, The Truth and The Life!

POEM 2

The Battle

"Everyone is resilient when it come to their beliefs, whether they be good or bad!"
Quoted by Dederick Woodard

Most people in life think that the battle is between good and evil, and for most cases that is true. But I dare to challenge you to seek to consider a different perspective, and that one that addresses the manifestation of that good or evil. You see it's one thing to have a good or an evil thought, but it's another thing to bring those thoughts to life. I call it "The Here to There Theory." The Here to

There theory is as simple as it seems, and simpler to bring to action. This theory is one that focuses on the process of getting from "here" to "there." One always represents the alpha zone and the other the omega zone, so that we can practice getting in something or out of something. I believe that the battle is to be or not to be is the one that most people find themselves battling, though there are many battles and we do fight them.

The process of getting from here to there.

Get out of my head is a common phrase that most people tend to communicate with their ideas, but for some reason they do not seem to be speaking the same language. Here is a little example of a conversation between my ideas and my moment.

The conversation:
1:
Idea: wouldn't it be nice to have some ice-cream right now!
Moment: look around we are at work, and who do you think wants to see you eating ice-cream!

2:
Idea: Man, she is hot, she is making me want to have some ice-cream right now, I wonder where she is from?

Moment: look around we are at an ice-cream shop, and that's why we came here in the first place to get some ice-cream right!

Two separate conversations and both could be evil or good, but both are identifying the relationship between purpose and position. First where are you and then what is the purpose of you being there. Secondly where would you like to be and how would you get there? As we can clearly see the "Idea" and the "Moment" have two different focuses. "The Idea" is a dreamer and is always dreaming about something, and "The Moment" is goal oriented and is always about getting things done. As we began to study and understand the difference between the two we will begin to see how to place them on one accord more often as often as possible.

Now the Idea and the Moment are two parts of a bigger team, and there is another required in the process to get from here to there. I will reveal the others parts later but just know that their is more than meets the eye, and each part must work with the other as a team to make the dream work. A team has specific partners that are required to bring the desired goal to life, and this is very important to know when you are apart of a team because it says that, "you are here for a reason!"

As we look again at the Idea and the Moment, one representing the dream and the other representing the manifestation of dreams, we can begin to look a little closer than the surface of this battle to see clearly what this battle is for.

THOUGHTS TO PLUNDER

Time and Space

Tell me of a Time, tell me of a place and I will show you the location of opportunity and the time to experience that opportunity!

A quote by Dederick Woodard

It's a difference between being in the right place versus being in the right time. Knowing the difference between the two and having the know-how to allow them to be on one Accord will allow you to connect preparation with opportunity!
A quote by
Dederick Woodard

"MY ATMOSPHERE"

What will I be in it; will I be a **"Monitor"** or a **"Moderator?"** As we know a monitor only displays what it see, but a moderator conducts and instructs what it desires to see. So, now knowing this, I ask myself this; Which one will I be, and the answer can only be told by time, as

time tells me in the moment what it perceives!

A Thought to Plunder

by

Dederick Woodard

Switching Gears, AKA Upgrade You

It's one thing to be a dreamer, and Dream Big Dreams

or, you can Dream a Little Dream, the size of the

dream does not matter, the point is to dream!

Dreams are in our heads and they exist there and the

reality of our mind as possible moments, but mostly

dreams are just thoughts. Now, to switch gears, to transcend from the dream world to the living world, or the world of the living a dream must go on the journey of the goal!

The goal is to required path for the dream to become a reality!

The dream Realm requires psychological effort to exist and develop, and the goal Realm requires physical effort to exist and develop. Yeah, the way we switch gears from the dream Realm to the Gold Realm is to Simply transform thinking into doing. In 2003 I was blessed to write a song call "Do as God Do," and this song exposes the transition that I speak of which is this: " think it, speak it, do as God do, remember; the God that died resides in you , think it, speak it, live cause God lives, put some actions to those words that you spill!" Yes, it's one thing to put an idea into thoughts which is psychological action and have a dream and it's a whole nother thing to put those thoughts into physical action and have an experience! I realized that I must be committed to placing my dreams where they need to go so that they can exist in the goal Realm and become a part of the reality realm!

The dream 🌎 is a playground to transform your known world.

For example I will utilize a word you know to teach you the definition of words you may have not considered before.

We'll start with the word "Futuristic" which allows us to assume that something is advance. So from that we will look at the words: "Presentistic" and "Pastistic." Presentistic would paint the picture that something is really made for right now. Pastistic would paint the picture of something that would have been useful in your past.

Now here, we utilize the word futuristic to have dreams to become reality. I dreamed of two other words and I utilize the word futuristic to help those words to become a part of the reality within your mind thus Switching gears.

It's like being on the two way street of influence, and one way is the "influencer" and the other is the "influencee." The influencer is the teacher and the "influencee" is the student . You see in every situation influence is always apart of the atmosphere. It's up to us to decide what side of the street of influence we're going to be on or what side do we find ourselves on while in the situation that we find ourselves in! Now, like me you have probably heard, pick a side, well, first before we pick a side, I learned that I must first identify what side of the street of influence I am on. Now, that I understand what side of the street of influence I am on, I can accurately identify and apply what's needed to arrive on the side of the street of influence that I desire to be on while in that situation.

Thus, Switching gears! We switch gears by receiving or releasing influence. When we switch gears we go from dreaming to goaling. As We Know, dreaming allows ideas to exist in the reality of our minds, and goaling allows ideas to exist in the reality of our moments!

Now, to understand and apply influence when it comes to these two realities of the dream in the goal, we must be aware of when we are addressing the reality of the dream which is the thought realm or the realm of possibilities, or addressing the reality of the goal which is the realm of manifestation of experiences. Okay, this time we are going to switch gears utilizing the same word twice to upgrade ourselves from the dream Realm to the goal Realm. Now, as you remember in my previous book discover you we talked about chronological time and geographical location, here I will show you how they can be separate and one in the same. Have you ever heard of the word present? Or have you ever heard of the word present? Let me help you, I know that it sounded like I said the same thing twice, but I actually said two separate things. Let's look again at the word present. What I learned from this word, is that the way we break it down is how it builds us up. Let's start in the dream Realm. To present something to someone is to offer something, example, ladies and gentlemen I would like to present to you the new 2020 BMW! This is something that will probably be offered to you by the owner of a BMW dealership like someone maybe named Victor Young. Now present this idea being me and not him, I would have to utilize my imagination or be in the dream reality. Now let's switch gears and upgrade this dream into an experience. First, I would have to place this dream into the path of the goal so that it can transfigure into a reality. To do this, I must first find Mr. Victor Young and ask him when can he make this dream a reality by allowing it to become a part of a moment? Then when he says yes, we must identify that moment, so that it is no longer a futuristic idea and it becomes a part of that moment of that event, that we call right now during that event or during that moment we can call it the present! So, to Simply show Switching gears or upgrading I thought process utilizing the word present twice, we can say this, I would love for you to present this BMW to me Mr. Victor Young right now in the present! Now, let's look at the words: present (Pres-ent) deals with a person being in a particular place, and present (Pre-sent) deal with giving someone something ceremonially. As you can see it's all in how you break it down.

Remember dreams deal with hope and the possibilities of Hope. Goals deal with faith, in the manifestation of faith. Now, you can hope and dream but to Hope and dream Without Love or the manifestation of love which is charity allows that hope or that faith to not reach its full potential or it's accurate destination! As you know in 1st Corinthians chapter 13 it exposes the power of partnering with love or the manifestation of love which is called charity. When

Hope partners with charity it can transition into faith, this is how dreams transition and two goals, which is through charity. Remember, remember, remember it was in a song by Paul McCartney and John Lennon in which they said "all we need is love love love all we need is love!"

"A Hidden Treasure"

I know that you have heard of this phrase: "Get the mind and the body will follow!" Well, I was taught by the Holy Spirit that same thing. I was shown that when I get the mind of Jesus Christ the body of Jesus Christ will follow.

So, once I activate what Paul said in Philippians 2:5, when he said "Let this mind be in you, which was also in Christ Jesus," by doing so exposed a system that we can apply as a strategy to produce divine solutions. If you ever see a minister having challenges with a body of Christ, please be encouraged to encourage them to ask The Holy Spirit to equip them with the Mind of Christ need for the body of Christ that they are addressing to equip them with the need resources that God The Father of Lights has sent them to do. Remember that your attitude will affect your altitude, yes how you handle yourself on the inside can definitely determine how far you go out and up.

So, how do I make sure that I am in the right place at the right time, and that I am doing the right thing at the right time to receive the right thing at the right time? Answer: I don't! My job is to allow the Holy Spirit to Have the mind of Christ to assist me in perceiving my position correctly, to respond correctly to produce what God Most High desires with my moment and position. In other words: One mind, to arrive at one place to be on one accord to usher in the Holy Spirit! We can prepare a place, if we are open to hearing how, even if that place is the position that we find ourselves in. Now, the secret to doing what Moses did when he saw the burning bush, is to do what Paul says and that is to put on the mind of Christ Jesus.

Doing this will equip us to hear from the higher Wisdom which comes from the mouth of God, and as we all know it's one thing to have information and it's another thing to understand and apply it. Applying it will develop our might and understanding it will place us in positions to be mighty with that wisdom! I realized that I can be called and choose to answer the call or not. Now, once I realize that I am chosen and answer the call I will learn what I need to do to be faithful, but once I do what is required to be faithful I will be know as I am known by my love which in this case will be the Love of Christ Jesus.

Doing this allows The Holy Spirit to become our mentor so that it can;

- See the potential within us,
- Expect the best out of us, and
- Express it's belief in us to produce what The Lord God desires to release through us.

This is done to expose what areas they can show and share to recruit others and develop and grow!

Did that Encourage you to Remember The Chapter:
"Second Time Around"

Where is Your Focus?

Part 1: "The Issue"

I noticed that there are two things that you can focus on in your situation; 1st on the "Fault," 2nd on the "Fix!" I realized that you can either focus on what made it happen or what can happen to make it better. Now, as we know I have been utilized to share things is a two step system. You see, people don't know who you are even if they know what type of issue you are in, remember you are not the issue that you are addressing; and you can be molded by the issue, or the issue can be molded by you. I have learned that I can focus on the "Fault," the "Fix," or neither! Now, believe it or not there have been many times in my life that I found myself just drifting through life, not allowing the issues to sway me one way or another. On the other hand, when it did give attention to my issues, my energy either went to blaming someone or something or building a solution. Again, focusing on the "Fault" or the "Fix!" I realized that focusing on the "Fault" only brought emotional excitement, and that soon after faded to nothing. Now, on the other hand, when I focused on what was needed to "Fix" it, I found emotional excitement and physical resolution. As time went on I realized that when I focused on the solution and "Fixed" my efforts on manifesting that solution life for me as I knew it changed. Now, knowing this I have a platform to see myself from that will give me perspective and that platform is: Am I moving from a Fault Mindset or from a Fix Mindset? I can utilize my hands to point fingers and find "Fault" or I can utilize my hands to "Fix" the situations by finding solutions!

Part 2: "Them, or They?"

I know that you might be like, "What does he mean, "Them, or They?"" Well, let me explain, it is just that, the question that you might have presented, what does anyone mean when they say, "Them or They?" I know for me it helps me to respond in greater accuracy when I know that "Them or They" is referring to a group of people standing on the other side of the room, or even me and the group that I am with.

All I am saying is that it is always better for everyone involved to know who the "Them or They" is when hearing information. Because if we do not know who "Them or They" is we cannot make the shift and go from talking about them to talking to them, from talking to them to talking with them. It's always been a process for me, because it's always been easier to talk to Mister or Misses than to talk to a Mystery!

Now, once we identify who "Them and They" are, we can go from theory to the here and now and bring forth the change that we desire to see. I realized that I can talk about "Them or They" all day and things can never change, but when I identify who "Them or They" is we can began to have discussions about the issues that we are concerned about and start working on solutions. When we know who "Them or They" is we can begin working on becoming "US!" I have learned that we all at one point in time have all been "Them or They," and once identified and communicated with, the opportunity to manifest the steps to becoming us always somehow seemed to present themselves. Some opportunities were easy to receive and other opportunities cost more than the price we were willing to pay to see the change that we desired.

A Thought to Plunder

By

Dederick Woodard

"Battle of the Views"

First View, The Outer View Perspective, this is a view that focuses on what's presented.

Presentation is everything when you say nothing and allow what you present to speak for you. It's like going to the mall dressed up and your finest Linens looking like a boss! When you walk into the store looking like a boss, most my assume that you are the boss based on their outer View of Who You Are.

Second View, is the Inner View Perspective, which allows someone to perceive how you perceive things. The InterView exposes one's morals and values and it also gives insight on how this person might agree or disagree with the views of the interviewer. Thus we have interviews, the playing field where the interviewer has the opportunity to understand and process the views of the interviewee.

A Thought to Plunder

By Dederick Woodard

Understanding the Perspectives of Understanding.

1. The finding ;

though it cost you everything get understanding. To get understanding is to Define a covering that you decide to be under so that you can develop, by identifying by developing and manifesting what you are under.

2. The connecting;

Once you identify the understanding that you desire to developing then you must connect with it. The connecting requires receiving the covering of the understanding that you want to be a part of.

3. The submitting;

To learn understanding it's to submit to what you want to understand. Submitting is committing and doing this will allow one to perform, so that your performance can be evaluated and enhanced. Becoming like the covering displays that you are gaining understanding.

4. The Manifesting;

When you manifest at the level of a master then others will come for understanding and place themselves in position to be students and disciples because you have gained understanding thus, you have become a covering for others!

A Thought to Plunder

By

Dederick Woodard

{The Goal(Cost) of a System is to transform, and the Gold(Value) of a Strategy is to transfigure!}

"Beyond Quotations"

By The Holy Spirit Sharing through Dederick Woodard

When systems transform into strategies and transfigure into realities everything changes. The Lord is beyond "Thoughts" and yet is The Alpha and Omega of them, When systems transform into strategies and transfigure into realities everything changes. The Lord is beyond "Words" and yet is The Alpha and Omega of them, When systems transform into strategies and transfigure into realities everything changes. The Lord is beyond "Actions" and yet is The Alpha and Omega of them, When systems transform into strategies and transfigure into realities everything changes. The Lord is beyond "Evaluations" and yet is The Alpha and Omega of them, When systems transform into strategies and transfigure into realities everything changes.

Something To Plunder

by

Dederick Woodard

No, Some, Any!

We have all heard someone say to us one of the following three words: No, Some, Any. Now, as simple as they might seem, they hold within them secrets of the universe! They are keys that open up the doors to locations and matter. For fun let's call the locations: where; and let's call the matter: things. I almost forgot, we exist in time, so door number 3 will deal with chronological time. So, let us begin the race of activating the keys. Key number 1, the "No" key, represents the closed minded. Key number 2, the "Some" key, represents the considering minded. Key number 3, the "Any" key, represents the open minded.

Location= Where, Door Number 1

Key Number 1

If we put key number 1 into the "Where Door," we would find ourselves going "nowhere," which is really funny to me because no-where can also mean that you are now-here! Get it, you don't have to move because you don't have to go nowhere because you are now-here! It's a dead end door. This is a key that unlocks closed things, that will only get you nowhere!

Key Number 2

If we put key number 2 into the "Where Door," we would find ourselves going "somewhere," which is an upgrade because we are going from nowhere to somewhere. Now, if you have not noticed yet, to go from nowhere to somewhere is progress! Yet, we are not where we want to be, we are moving forward. Things tend to move forward when we work with considering minded people, but there is always another level of greater access.

Key Number 3

Now, as we utilize key number 3 into the "Where Door," we find ourselves going "anywhere," which is the ultimate experience. Imagine having access to anywhere, how would that affect your response to others around you? How big would you dream? Would it be enough to take the limits off of where you believe you can go within the physical, the educational, the psychological or the spiritual?

Matter=Thing, Door Number 2

<u>Key Number 1</u>

As we activate key number 1, with the "Thing Door," we will come to realize that it will get us "nothing!" Billy Preston said, "Nothing from nothing leaves nothing, and you have to have something if you wanna be with me," he went from key number 1 to key number 2 just like that, so we will do the same. You see closed minded people will take you for all you got and in return give you "Nothing!"

Key Number 2

Now, Key number 2, connecting with the "Thing Door," shifts gears for us and give us the something zone. This is the place where things can happen, or at least be considered. Minds here are at least taking the time to process things, and processing can lead to producing. Now, this can sometimes lead to a thing.

Key Number 3

Yes! Imagine being able to do anything and have anything, because everyone you meet is an open minded person.

Door Number 3, Time=Moments

Key Number 1

No time erases all opportunities, because when someone is closed minded to an opportunity you will have no moments.

Key Number 2

Who wants to almost have a moment, to meet the person of their dreams? Who wants to stay in the consideration zone when it comes to something that is important to them? Not me, but if that is you I am not mad at you, I actually want to say thank you for giving others more moments to connect to.

Key Number 3

Yes! Any moment, at anytime! WOW! This is living life with full expectation. Here dreams are goals because here we move within the moments. Open minded people move when the time is right. Moment are for making, and making is a platform for dreams to become goals within the moments, and here we have anytime all we have to do is activate it!

Remember:

Key Number 1: There is nowhere for nothing, because there is no-time.

Key Number 2: There is somewhere for something, because there is sometime.

Key Number 3: There is anywhere for anything, because we can utilize anytime.

A Thought to Plunder

by

Dederick Woodard

"The Power of the Voice"

There is a power found within the location of the voice that is known, and their voice itself is a power all to itself as well.

There are 3 levels of addressing the voice that will be shared here today.

-Level -1: The Mindset of the beast No Voice

-Level 0: The Mindset of God Most High (Upper Inner Voice)

-Level +1: The Mindset of Man (Lower Inner Voice)

Level (-1) is the level that has no inner voice and only submits and connects with a voice of a creation that presents a greater strength than itself. The commands that it appears to display is flight or fight, which is to run or get down, you decide. Here in this mindset it is either a lets get it or a lets go reality. Here there are few opportunities to talk, it's more of an action platform.

Level (+1) is a creation that has self awareness which is this situation is called the inner voice. This inner voice bestows upon us self awareness, which transcends them beyond the platform of flight and fight to a platform of collaboration and coexisting. This might create an

"I am better than you mindset," that might cause a challenge. Here in this mindset, most believe that they have all the answers or can find them, so they try to impress their perspective on those around them. Now, because all creations have different beliefs, those beliefs will shape those collaborations and coexisting, which might or might not be fair for all parties.

Level (0) is a creation that has acquired the upper voice, which expresses the power of influence which comes from the Spiritual Realm. For me my Level (0) is connecting with the Most High God through Christ which makes me a offspring and a child which is beyond a creation. A child had been endowed with the abilities to move and respond with the abilities of the Parents, and in this case parents are Father God Most High and Mother earth. In this platform Level (1) and Level (-1) can find this platform of connect and become Level (0) as we that live on this Level (0) love those who are willing to receive this love into this level.

In the bible, I learned that the Spirit which to me is level (0) assists me in times when I find myself a level (-1) or level (+1) to balance out to level (0) to move and respond at maximum capacity for the full duration.

A Thought to Plunder

by

Dederick Woodard

3 Eyed Monster or Master?

What is a 3 Eyed Monster? What is a 3 Eyed Master? Well, to me it is 3 Different ways of seeing something, and a Monster sees one way and a Master sees another way.

There are 3 ways that the Monster and the Master perceive things and Master has 1 extra way of seeing that helps it to master the monster. Below are the three ways of seeing that we will expose:
- The Natural Eye (60 degrees),
- The Mind's Eye (60 degrees), and
- The Emotional Eye (60 degrees).

All "Try-Angles" equal 180 degrees, get it: try-angles, they require mental and physical effort.

The fourth way of seeing the 1 extra way will be shared later in this section labeled *Bonus!*

The Natural Eye

What is the Natural Eye Concept? To answer that question we must look at the simple fact that the natural eye is just that, your natural eye! It is what it is and somethings are just as simple as they seem, but most of the time we tend to look deep into things when we just need to see them for what they are and allow their fruit to encourage us to look further. The Natural Eye addresses the two eyes that we utilize to perceive the world around us. The Monster utilize those eyes to identify what to destroy and defeat, while The Master utilize those eyes to identify what to deliver and defeat. Now, while the Monster focuses on what to destroy and the Master focuses on what to deliver, they both are still united on what to defeat to make that 1st goal possible. Have you every built something like a sandcastle and when you were filled with joy and ready to share it with those that you loved, someone "The Monster" destroyed your castle attempting to defeat the joy that dwelled within you? Now, on the other hand, have you every built something like a sandcastle and when someone came to destroy it, had someone "The Master" deliver you from "The Monster" and defeating them and saving the day? So, from these two situations we can see that "The Monster" is designed to destroy the way you see the world around you with your natural eye, and "The Master" is designed to deliver you from being destroyed by defeating "The Monster." It's a battle between "The Monster" and "The Master" to address how you utilize your natural eye to see the world around you.

The Mind's Eye

How does the Mind have an Eye? How can a person see something that is not there? I respond to both of those questions by saying, " to see something that others cannot see you must have perspective, and sometimes that requires us to see something in our minds before we can perceive them within our moments. In simple words our "Minds Eye" is our imagination! The job of "The Monster" is to encourage us to perceive from the platform of FEAR, and "The Master" has the job to encourage us to perceive form the platform of FAITH. Fear will paralyze you and Faith will propel you. As shared before as we think or utilize our imagination and this sets the stage for our "Will Power." "The Monster" wills power to use FEAR to sit you down, while "The Master" wills power to use FAITH to get you going, and being that all things start in the mind be reminded that "The Mind's Eye" for us is the Alpha and the Omega for us as it pertains to shifting our paradigms. If I were to say imagine an apple to a group of 100 plus people, their is a slight chance that everyone might not see the same color apple. Some, might see a green apple, some a yellow apple and others a bright red apple! But those who put forth effort to activate their "Mind's Eye" would perceive an apple as never seen before by the others with their "Natural Eye" before as they activate their imagination. Example: A Golden Apple! Made of Real Gold! That you can EAT! Imagine that!

The Emotional Eye

This eye, "The Emotional Eye" addresses our attitude, and as we know "your attitude determines your altitude," something I learned from John Maxwell who is a global leader developer. "The Monster" utilizes all emotions that lead you to and keep you performing on the stage of FEAR, while "The Master" on the other hand; utilizes all emotions to lead you to and keep you performing on the stage of FAITH! "The Monster" is designed to keep your out of control, while "The Master" is designed to assist you in developing self-control, that's being in control. Being out of control, sets the stage of being a victim, while being in control sets the stage of being a victor! Your dereve to win, but no matter how much the world around us shares that with us, it is meaningless unless we share it with ourselves first and believe it!

Bonus
What makes "The Master" the master is that it has a factor to assist it in controlling "The Monster," which is "The Spirit!" Now, for some, they might connect with

whatever spirits that get them emotionally aroused, but for me I am striving to connect with "The Most High Spirit" and the only one that I can do it with maximum access is to do it through Christ Jesus. This allows me to start from "The Won Position" as I walk out "The Win" in my moment or situation. As Christ said, "It is Finished!"

The difference of Lights

Today, I Learned that there is a light that is used to see and there is a light that is utilized to perceive! Now, as we understand and apply the difference between the two lights we will increase what we see as well as also increase what we perceive. For me to see addresses things in the natural and in the physical and to perceive addresses things and the spiritual and the psychological!

1) When I look with my eye (Natural Light) what do I see? Do I see opportunities or do I see opposition's? (COST- what's required)

2) When I look to perceive with my mind's eye (Spiritual Light) what do I see? What do I see opportunities or do I see opposition's? (VALUE-meaning or importance to me or someone else)

TUNNEL VISION

Tunnel vision requires you: to be able to have a perspective; while you're traveling through the tunnel. Thus, the name tunnel vision! A prospective is just a way: of seeing something. A tunnel can be a situation: where when you look to the left and yet you see nothing; when you look to the right you see nothing; and will you look up if you can see nothing, but when you look ahead to see the end, you see a light, and tunnel vision is being able to focus on that light until you arrive in that light!

A Thought to Plunder By Dederick Woodard

"Seed Systems and Seed Strategies"

Knowing the difference between the systems and the strategies allow those who have this special information to:

"Switch Gears!"

**I used to be a Dreamer Dreaming Dreams,
now I'm living them,
Checking off every gold on my list, yeah I'm killing them,
Manifesting every goal in my head, yeah I'm building them,
Blueprints from my mind to them blocks, I'm fa' feeling them!**

Now as we drive we know how to perceive one gear from the next and also how the gears work together. What does it mean to switch gears? Switching gears means that more is required to reach fulfillment, and there is more than meets your moment, meaning your ear must hear more, your eye must see more and your body must do more! Here I will utilize a 3 gear process that goes from systems to strategies.

Remember My Goal is to display that:

"it's a Difference Between:

A) Pronouncing my Passions, and

B) Pursuing my Passions!"

"1st Gear"
Identifying The Difference
A) Pronouncing My Passions:

In this gear will meet what I like to call the know it all spirit. In this state I found myself having so much to say and little to nothing to do. Imagine having the answer to everything with little to no effort when it comes to applying that amazing knowledge. This is the part that focuses on **"Pronouncing my Passions!"** It is the fullness of the point concept which is to activate the system. I call this first gear the "Perspective Position." I call this "HEAD Knowledge," In this gear all we do is see, and I do mean see because we see potential and possibilities without limitations! In this zone, the 1st Gear Zone; we can clearly see the difference between one thing from the other. I realized that when I am in this state I am nothing more than talk, and yet sometimes talk is enough and other times it's too cheap to buy action.

Remember Action Cost, and that cost is EFFORT! Knowledge is all about seeing with your internal eyes and external eyes! R-Kelly said it in the song "I Believe I Can Fly" that: "If I can see it, than I can do it," so I know that perception brings possibilities, and possibilities bring with them hope! We can perceive good things, bad things, nice things or nasty things and nevertheless we will perceive things. Having a knowledge about something but no visual, is like having a dead faith. So, when I find myself in this position I realize that I need to switch gears.

"2nd Gear"
Exposing The Difference
B) Pursuing My Passions:

R-Kelly also said the same song that: "If I just believe it there's nothing to it!" ACTION, ACTION, ACTION, in other words, *effort!* "Effort is the Difference," and watching someone do something displays possibilities! I call this "HEEL Knowledge" When I see possibilities being displayed I find myself having a great desire to start: **"Pursuing My Passions!"** It is the fullness of the play concept which address activating the strategy. When someone is walking out something, it takes me from the hope phase into the faith realm. It's allows us to see faith alive. Now, who wants to see something that they do not understand, especially if they have a desire to reproduce it! Have you ever ate a meal and after realizing that it was the most amazing thing that you have ever experienced. I don't know about you but I would have to know how it is done. Now, to know requires communication. When faith becomes a visual mystery we need to do something different. So, again I find myself in a position where I need to switch gears.

"3rd Gear"
Experiencing The Difference:

Let's do it, and do it in a way where we can do it again and again! "3rd Gear" derives from a platform that is hidden within a book of the Bible called James, and within the 2nd chapter of that book, where it breaks down 1st gear and 2nd gear. This is what it looks like when you bring the point and play together, point meaning system and play meaning strategy.

James 2: 17-18

"17 Even so faith, if it hath not works, is dead, being alone.

18 Yea, a man may say, Thou hast faith, and I have works: shew me thy faith without thy works, and I will shew thee my faith by my works."

In this 3rd gear we can see the knowledge of finding life and the effort each alone is dead, but the effort connecting with life in the knowledge creates a living faith! I call this "<u>HEAL Knowledge</u>," This 3rd gear allows actions to reproduce after their own kind. In other words effort brings power to knowledge, or we can just say its the strategy that applies the system of switching gears! Here we connect the 1st Gear (HEAD Knowledge) which is what you say with 2nd Gear (HEEL Knowledge) which what you do, to produce 3rd Gear (HEAL Knowledge) which is to do what you say and to say what you do!

Remember this: I love peanut-butter cookies, and it's one thing to read about them, which will leave them dead to my stomach but to read the receipt and to prepare them for me displays a living faith that will bring praise! Now, this idea works for anything that anyone desires, so learn how to do and also how to share it. This places you in a position to meet the needs of those who desire to have this experience, and as you teach others to follow in your footsteps through them you can have leverage and reproduce after your own kind!

CHAPTER 9
SOWING GREATNESS FORWARD

I have learned that there are ways of sowing greatness, and a way to sow that greatness forward. My goal through this book and my presentations have been to equip those that are in my presence with this reality. Below are three things to focus on that I pray will assist you in presenting that greatness.

1st A Prayer, 2nd A Psalms and 3rd A Proverbs.

The Prayer
Daily Weekly Prayer

Saturday S.O.L.
A time to focus and learn about who the Father is so that we can know who we are it is the nucleus of it all (Revelation 4 all)
Command the alpha part of my day (Pray 1st watch for S.O.L. 6-6am)
A central element around which other elements are grouped

Sunday S.O.W.
We start by focusing on the wisdom of the Father that we understand and then move in to the wisdom that we do not understand because we want to go deeper into His Presence so we call out for insight and cry aloud for understanding to show up in our new day
Command the alpha part of my day (Pray 2nd watch for S.O.W. 6pm-9pm)

Monday S.O.U.
We walk in the faith that the Lord has given us His Spirit of Understanding so we use this understanding to discover what kind of council or counsel we need so we call out for insight and cry aloud for understanding of what kind of council or counsel we need to show up in our new day
Command the alpha part of my day (Pray 3rd watch for S.O.U. 9pm-1030pm)

Tuesday S.O.C.
Walking in the faith that the Lord has given me His council/counsel and use that council/counsel to see what type of might He needs me to walk in so I call out for insight and cry aloud for understanding of that might to show up in my new day
Command the alpha part of my day (Pray 4th watch for S.O.C. 1030pm to 12am)

Wednesday S.O.M.
Walk in the faith that the Lord has given me His Might and use the Might to see what type of Knowledge He wants me to walk in

so I call out for insight and cry aloud for understanding of the knowledge to show up in my new day

Command the alpha part of my day (Pray 5th watch for S.O.M. 12am-3am)

Thursday S.O.K.

Walking in the faith that the Lord has given me His Knowledge and use that knowledge to see what type of Reverence/fear of Him I need to walk in so I call out for insight and cry aloud for understanding of that Reverence/Fear of Him to show up in my new day

Command the alpha part of my day (Pray 6th watch for S.O.K. 3am- 430am)

Friday S.O.F.

Walking in the faith that the Lord has given me His Reverence/Fear of Him and use that Reverence/Fear to enter into His Presence and to see How He wants me to walk in His Presence so I call out for insight and cry aloud for understanding of His Presence to show up in my new day

Command the alpha part of my day (Pray 7th watch for S.O.F. 430am-6am)

The Psalm
A Psalm of Dederick Woodard
Psalm 3

1 Lord, because you chose to lay down your life to pick it up in me I have your Spirit Lord it leads me to your wisdom; and now because I have within me you Lord I can walk in your wisdom,

2 and your wisdom leads me to deeper understanding of who you are, and because you have placed your wisdom within me I now am able to walk in that understanding which is to

me knowledge of who you are to me and for me,

3 and this deeper understanding of who you are to me Lord leads me to desiring your counsel/council, and now because your understanding which in you and because you have placed yourself within me I now am able to walk in that council/counsel,

4 which is a council/counsel that leads me to your might/power which is incomprehensible without you, so because you have placed your

council/counsel within me I am able to walk within your might/power,

5 and your incomprehensible might/power leads me and guides me to your knowledge which is what you used to create all that is and will be, so I bless you and thank you for placing your incomprehensible might/power within me so that I am enabled with you and by you to walk in your knowledge which is inconceivable in the natural mind of men,

6 and this knowledge which is inconceivable within my own strength that you blessed me to walk in leads me to a greater reverence of you Lord, so for this I thank you for placing it within me this knowledge so that I may walk in the reverence of who you are,

7 because walking in reverence of who you are brings forth this child that belongs to you into your presence, and brings forth your presence to your child, and now because I whom you have claimed as your child have within me the

reverence of who your are I can walk within you presence,

8 and walking your presence leads me to your Seven Spirits, and because you have placed within me your presence I can walk in your Seven Spirits in a every increasing measurements.

The Proverb
<u>8/11/07 10:45am blessing</u>

From the Holy Spirit through Dederick D Woodard

1 Because I have the Spirit of the Lord (Presence of the Lord) it leads me to the Wisdom of the Lord, and now because I have within me the Spirit of the Lord (Presence of the Lord) I walk in the Wisdom of the Lord.

2 The Wisdom of the Lord leads me to the Understanding of the Lord, and Now because I have the Wisdom of the Lord within me I walk-in the Understanding of the Lord which is Knowledge of the Holy One.

3 The Understanding of the Lord leads me to the Council/Counsel of the Lord, and now because I have the Understanding of the Lord within me I walk in the Council/Counsel of the Lord.

4 The Council/Counsel of the Lord lead me to the Might/Power of the Lord, and now because I have the Council/Counsel of the Lord within me I walk in the Might/Power of the Lord.

5 The Might/Power of the Lord lead to the Knowledge of the Lord, and now because I have the Might/Power of the Lord Within me I walk in the Knowledge of the Lord.

6 The Knowledge of the Lord leads to the Reverence of the Lord, and now because I have the Knowledge of the Lord within me, I walk-in the Reverence of the Lord.

7 The Reverence of the Lord leads to the Spirit of the Lord (Presence of the Lord), and now because I have within me the Reverence of the Lord I walk in the Spirit of the Lord (Presence of the Lord),

8 Because I have within me the Seven Spirits of the Lord I walk-in the Seven Spirits of the Lord.

The rest of this page is Blank on purpose, this is how we need to start every opportunity!

"Secrets hidden since the foundations of the Word!"

Matthew 13:35
This was to fulfill what was spoken through the prophet: "I will open My mouth in parables; I will utter things hidden since the foundations of the world."
Parable:
Level 1: Mark 4:1-9
Location:
Mark 4:1-2 And again He began to teach by the sea. And a great multitude was gathered to him, so that he got into a boat and sat in it on the sea; and the whole multitude was on the land facing the sea. Then he taught them many things by parables, and said to them in His teachings;

Sower 1 Part A
Mark 4:3-4 "Listen! Behold, a Sower went out to sow. And it happened as he sowed, that some seed fell by the wayside (Location); and the birds of the air came and devoured it (attack).

SOWER 1 PART B

MARK 4:14-15 THE SOWER SOWS THE WORD. AND THESE ARE THE ONES BY THE WAY SIDE WHERE THE WORD IS SOWN. WHEN THEY HEAR, SATAN COMES IMMEDIATELY AND TAKES AWAY THE WORD THAT WAS SOWN IN THEIR HEARTS.

OVERVIEW:

HERE WE ARE EXPOSED TO THE REALITY THAT A SOWER SOWS SOMETIMES BY JUST TOSSING IT OUT THERE. HERE THAT LOCATION IS CALLED THE WAYSIDE, AND SATAN OR HIS EMPTS ARE CALLED BIRDS OF THE AIR COME AND TAKES THE WORD AWAY THAT WAS SOWN IN YOUR HEART. THIS IS DONE IF YOU DO NOT GUARD YOUR HEART, BY PUTTING ON THE ARMOR OF GOD. YOU MUST ALSO TAKE EVERY THOUGHT (WHICH COME FROM WHAT YOU HEAR) CAPTIVE AND SUBMIT IT UNTO THE MIND OF CHRIST. CHRIST STARTS OF BY SAYING "LISTEN! BEHOLD," BECAUSE IF YOU HEAR WITH YOUR EARS AND UNDERSTAND AND SEE WITH YOUR EYES AND PERCEIVE AND TURN HE WILL HAVE TO HEAL YOU. AND BEING HEALED WILL STOP YOU FROM BEING DESTROYED.

Parable of the Seed Exposed from a Divine Perceptive

Sower 2 Part A

Mark 4:5-6 Some fell on stony ground, where it did not have much earth (Location); and immediately it sprang up because it had no depth of earth (reaction). But when the sun was up it was scorched, and because it had no root it was withered away (attack).

Sower 2 Part B

Mark 4:16-17 These likewise are the ones sown on stony ground who, when they hear the word, immediately receive it with gladness; and they have no root in themselves, and so endure only for a time. Afterward, when tribulation or persecution arises for the word's sake, immediately they stumble.

Overview:

When the Word falls on stony ground or broken ground means that it was heard and received with gladness and gave hope. But because it was no root within, no personal relationship, tribulations and persecution make us stumble. So we must allow the word to take root so that our tribulations and persecutions can increase the value of the harvest that will come because of the word. Remembering that every word has a hidden agenda will give us strength to hold on to it until is manifests.

Parable of the Seed Exposed from a Divine Perceptive

Sower 3 Part A
Mark 4:7 And some seed fell among thorns (Location); and the thorns grew up and choked it (ATTACK), and it yielded no crop (reaction).

Sower 3 Part B
Mark 4:18-19 Now these are the ones sown among thorns; they are the ones who hear the word, and the cares of this world, the deceitfulness of riches, and the desires for other things entering in choke the word, and it becomes unfruitful.

OVERVIEW:
IMAGINE HAVING A GREAT WORD AND ALLOWING THE THINGS AROUND YOU TO TAKE YOUR FOCUS OFF YOUR DELIVERANCE HERE ITS CALLED THE CARES OF THIS WORLD. WE SHOULD BE FOCUSED ON THE WORLD TO COME, REMEMBERING THAT THE LORD CAN HARVEST THE THORNS WITH THE WHEAT AND TOSS ON INTO THE FIRE AND SEPARATING ONE FROM THE OTHER. TAKING YOUR FOCUS OFF OF THE WORD CHOKES IT OUT AND MAKES YOU UNFRUITFUL, BUT FOCUSING ON THE WORD AND INCREASING YOUR FOCUS ON IT INCREASES YOUR FRUITFULNESS. SO, SEEK YE FIRST THE KINGDOM OF GOD AND ALL HIS RIGHTEOUSNESS AND ALL THESE THINGS WILL BE ADDED TO YOU.

PARABLE OF THE SEED EXPOSED FROM A DIVINE PERCEPTIVE

SOWER 4 PART A
MARK 4:8 BUT OTHER SEED FELL ON GOOD GROUND (LOCATION) AND YIELDED A CROP THAT SPRANG UP, INCREASED AND PRODUCED (REACTION); SOME THIRTYFOLD, SOME SIXTY, AND SOME A HUNDRED (TYPES OF HARVEST)."

Mark 4:9 And He said to them, "He who has ears to hear, let him hear!"

Sower 4 Part B
Mark 4:20 But these are the ones sown on good ground, those who hear the word, accept it, and bear fruit: some thirtyfold, some sixty, and some a hundred."

<u>Overview:</u>
Identifying good ground will ensure that you yield a crop, and this can only happen by finding those that hear the word, accept it and bear fruit even if the harvest varies from time to time, from 30 fold, 60 fold or a hundred percent of what was sowed. Is it not good enough to be like your master! Different Faith levels will produce different harvests but it must follow this system from heaven. Systems like this system from heaven must be reproduced; (hear it, accept it and bear fruit at least 30-fold and as much as 100-fold.) Christ is urging us to hear to the point that He is proclaiming a healing for those who has ears to be healed and "let him hear!"

Parable of the Seed Exposed from a Divine Perceptive

Level 2:
Location Luke 7:11 a city called: Nain
Luke 8:4-8
Location
Luke 8:4 And when a great multitude had gathered, and they had come to Him from every city, He spoke by parable:

Sower 1 Part A
Luke 8:5 "A Sower went out to sow his seed. And as he sowed, some fell by the wayside (LOCATION); and it was trampled down, and the birds of the air devoured it (ATTACK).

Sower 1 Part B
Luke 8:11-12 "Now the parable is this: The seed is the word of God. Those by the wayside are the ones who hear; then the devil comes
and takes away the word out of their hearts,

LEST THEY SHOULD BELIEVE AND BE SAVED.

OVERVIEW:
GOD IS THE SOWER AND THE LORD CAME FROM HEAVEN TO COLONIZE EARTH, AND HAVING SUCH AN ABUNDANCE OF WORD, SOME FELL BY THE WAYSIDE, WHICH MEANS THAT THOSE THAT HEARD A WORD FROM GOD GOT ATTACKED BY SATAN AND HE TRIES TO TRAMPLE THE WORD AND TO ALLOW THE BIRDS OF THE AIR TO DEVOURED IT, SO THAT WE WOULD NOT BELIEVE IT AND BECOME SAVED BY THE WORD. THE WORD NEEDS TO TAKE ROOT IN OUR HEARTS BY US NOT ALLOWING IT TO BE TRAMPLED AND DEVOURED BY SATAN AND THE BIRDS OF THE AIR. DOING ALL THAT WE CAN TO KEEP IT FROM BEING TAKEN FROM WITHIN OUR HEART.

PARABLE OF THE SEED EXPOSED FROM A DIVINE PERCEPTIVE

SOWER 2 PART A
LUKE 8:6 SOME FELL ON ROCK (LOCATION); AND AS SOON AS IT SPRANG UP (REACTION), IT WITHERED AWAY BECAUSE IT LACKED MOISTURE (ATTACK).

Sower 2 Part B

Luke 8:13 But the ones on the rock are those who, when they hear, receive the word with joy; and these have not root, who believe for a while and in time of temptation fall away.

Overview:

When we find a new word that gives us a great joy we should wait for the Holy Spirit to sprang up like a spring for hydration to moisturize the word so that can allow the roots to develop and become stronger to believe for a while and will not fall away when temptation come will not fall away when it falls on the rock because the word without mercy and grace can destroy. Find hope and encouragement from the word to keep the joy that comes in trusting and adhering to the Lord's will for your moment.

Parable of the Seed Exposed from a Divine Perceptive

Sower 3 Part A
Luke 8:7 And some fell among thorns (LOCATION), and the thorns sprang up with it and choked it (ATTACK).

Sower 3 Part B
Luke 8:14 Now the ones that fell among thorns are those who, when they have heard, go out and are choked with cares, riches, and pleasures of this life, and bring no fruit to maturity.

Overview:
When trapped by thorns and feeling choked by the cares of this world do not allow them to stop you from producing when you go out with the word. Be strong and focused to bring the fruit at hand to maturity. Maturity is a place that you deserve to arrive with your goals and dreams, but most important of all it is a place that will reward you when you take the word of God there.

Remembering that the Mature Spirit give birth to the Spirit and the Spirit has fruit that will nourish you when it is allowed to be produced that will change your life.

Parable of the Seed Exposed from a divine Perceptive

Sower 4 Part A

Luke 8:8 But others fell on good ground (location), sprang up (reaction), and yielded a crop a hundredfold." (Type of harvest) When He had said these things He cried, "He who has ears to hear, let him hear!"

Sower 4 Part B

Luke 8:15 But the ones that fell on the good ground are those who, having heard the word with a noble and good heart, keep it and bear fruit with patience.

Overview:

Good ground is allowing those who has an ear to hear to let him hear. Bearing fruit can only happen with patience as your partner. To implement the word which a system you must

have a noble and good heart to assist you in keeping the word. Not just keeping it in thought, but also in communication and action as well. Yielding a crop a hundredfold
requires that we follow this system with the correct mindset and pureness of heart. The joy will make it sprang up and we must remember to allow it to take root from a noble perspective which will create a good heart so that we can find courage to keep it until it bears a fruit that can bless nations generation after generation.

Chapter 10
ABOUT THE AUTHOR

I have been labeled by my action, the ones that I have spoken of beforehand and other that speak of me after I have chosen to take action! Some call me: son, brother, dad, cousin, friend, teacher, student, minister, chief, thief, preacher, miracle worker, presenter, provider, producer, boy, man, courageous, coward, confident, crazy, cool, christian, disciple, and the list can and does go on and on, but the one I love the most is when I hear my God and Father in Heaven say:

"Well done, good and faithful servant; thou hast been faithful over a few things, I will make the ruler over many things: enter thou into the joy of thy Lord."

This comes from Matthew 25:23 in the Kings James version of the Bible.

I am Dederick Demond Woodard,
and it is no longer I who lives but Christ who lives in me, so me I keeps him more than close I keeps Him in me, cause God done sent His grace and truth through Jesus, done made away so He Don't ever Have to leave us.

Below is a Paper that I wrote about who I am becoming, when you see me let me know how I am doing.

Woodard, Dederick
African American History
Professor Packer, Jack C.

The Epistemology of Dederick Woodard
An African American Legend

The term epistemology is described as "the branch of philosophy that studies the nature of knowledge, its presuppositions and foundations, and it extent and validity," by American Heritage Dictionary of the English Language, Fourth Edition. Dederick Woodard is the first Artist Psychologist known to man. And what is an Artist Psychologist you might ask? Well, an artist psychologist is a person who not only trains artists, but also puts artists into positions where they learn to study and develop themselves by understanding themselves. So as we ask these questions about

Dederick Woodard we will better understand why he is an African American Legend.

As we study the philosophy that studies the nature of the knowledge of how Dederick Woodard became the man that we know, today we take a deeper look into what makes a man a legend. You might say why is this man labeled as a legend? The answer to that question is not found in books or speeches, but found in the hearts of those that have chosen to make greater than what he has become. Dederick Woodard has taken his mind to a level of unselfishness that allows him to be received on as many levels as he chooses to apply himself.

Mr. Woodard's origin of humbleness can be condensed into one specific moment in his life. Mr. Woodard was about in the sixth grade when his language arts teacher was giving his class a test. He was deeply focused on reading a Spider-Man comic book instead of trying to take the test that he didn't study for, and he didn't try to hide it like most people might have; instead, he chose to hold the comic book up and read it as if it was a newspaper. This started a chain reaction that humbled Mr. Woodard for the rest of his life, because this involved his mother who wasn't having such a hot day at work. She came in and asked the principal why was her son being suspended, and the reply encouraged her to ask Mr. Woodard to go into the room next door. Shortly afterward she followed with the same paddle that Mr. Woodard wouldn't allow the principal to use to give him two swings through and his mother commenced to give him what seemed like twenty to thirty at a rapid speed. Not only did it hurt physically but it also hurt mentally. It was more embarrassing than painful, because the door to the room that Mr. Woodard was in was cracked, and it was beginning to open slowly and people were looking and laughing behind their hands. This probably chastised Mr. Woodard more than the swings of the wood, because at this point in his life he made up his mind that he would do whatever it takes to never ever experience anything like this again. Fortunately this was the end of the rollercoaster ride of disobedience and was the first step in climbing the mountain of obedience; goodbye selfishness and hello unselfishness were expressed in his actions.

Now that you have a picture of the type of character that Mr. Woodard is determined to become and present you will be able to understand why he chose to become an Artist Psychologist in the first place. Mr. Woodard spent his whole life searching to discover what he could do to make himself a better and more efficient musical artist, and one day while listening to this man speaking about truly knowing something. The man was no one he really knew and to this day he can't really remember who he was, or where he came from, but what he said changed Mr. Woodard forever. Mr. Woodard said that it stuck in his mind as plain as a picture on the wall that "If you truly get something that is truly great you will desire to give it a way as much and as often as possible". Mr. Woodard expressed his desire to become a great musical artist, and said, "That everything that it costs me to get there I pray that I can train others to do it, and keep the position that they gain". Day after day Mr. Woodard trained himself to develop in the presentations of the ideas, because he wanted the people to enjoy his ideas. This forced him to do deep studies on presentation. He not only had to understand the how's and why's of presentation, but he actually had to develop and institute the psychology of presentation into what he choose to do for a living. So, as we all know, everything that is instituted into a society must be tested and proven before others believe it to be a truth.

Therefore, Mr. Woodard tested his theories on himself. He started in the living room of his house by testing the stamina of an artist and how it affects his or her presentations. At first he found that after an half an hour or so for himself he would start to decrease in his presentation. This, lead Mr. Woodard to the theory of presenting images instead of words, which allows him to double the length of his clarity with in his presentations. This for Mr. Woodard was something better than great, for he had made the breakthrough of a lifetime in the eyes of a musical artist. In spite of this great discovery Mr. Woodard found himself with in a great state of sadness, for he had made this great discovery with no one to share it with.

As a result, Mr. Woodard developed different processes to build the artist that he desired to help. The first one is called the alphabet game. This is an exercise where a person uses the alphabet as a foundation and with each letter they find a different word to describe a topic for a minimum of at least four bars. This will allow the person to take something that is abstract and make it concrete. The second exercise is the stamina test. This is an exercise where the artist would play a collection of instrumentals for as long as they can share and present an idea in a concept that others can understand. This is normally done where there is a recording device so that they can study and critic themselves. This allows the artist to listen to their delivery and it also gives them a chance to check for imagery. This enables the artist to not only see where they can improve, but to place an emphasis on the things that they enjoyed in their presentation.

So this gave birth to what Mr. Woodard has come to label as an Artist Psychologist. Now the part that makes Mr. Woodard a legend is kind of hard to describe, because this part is something that will be expressed as time reveals it. Sometimes through the eyes and ear of an artist, or maybe through the ears of a listener that hear the work that is done by an artist that has been through this training and desires to do something that will change the world that we know it today. Now I am a Dream Doer!

Dream Doers

Dream Doers

Dream Doers

Dream Doers

Dream Doers

Dream Doers

Dream Doers

Dream Doers

Dream Doers

Dream Doers

Made in the USA
Columbia, SC
01 August 2019